FAME'S TWILIGHT

FAME'S TWILIGHT

STUDIES OF NINE MEN OF LETTERS

BY

KENNETH NEWTON COLVILE

Essay Index Reprint Series

 BOOKS FOR LIBRARIES PRESS

FREEPORT, NEW YORK

First Published 1923
Reprinted 1970

STANDARD BOOK NUMBER:
8369-1703-0

LIBRARY OF CONGRESS CATALOG CARD NUMBER:
73-117771

PRINTED IN THE UNITED STATES OF AMERICA

CONTENTS:

FOREWORD.

THE revaluation, from time to time, of our lesser classics is one of the most necessary critical tasks, and the studies contained in this book are the outcome of an intimate acquaintance with the works named herein extending over a good many years. It is to such a re-examination of the manner and content of certain bodies of literary work, whose authors looked giants to their own contemporaries, that I have applied myself in the ensuing pages.

In this I do not think I have disobeyed Arnold's precepts—not to be led astray by historical considerations but to apply to everything the touchstone of the absolutely highest and best. Fashions in literature pass and reputations with them, but the reputations not always deservedly. Many writers are admired in their lifetime for the wrong reason, but the disproving of their early admirers' claims should not debar them from having the same chance as the slower start-

ers of a fame based on more solid grounds.
Again, subsequent unanimity as to the pre-
eminence of a supremely great artist should
not preclude the recognition of a certain
though lesser degree of genius in his defeat-
ed rival. Nor where an art has fallen almost
into disuse should we forget its greatest
practitioners in the past. Occasionally, too,
a fashion revives, and it is interesting and
salutary to note the prototypes of its contemporary exponents, their brief glory, their
long oblivion.

A poet friend once came upon me reading
a poet of the day before yesterday and re-
proved me for spending so much time on out-
worn specimens of the art he himself practised. I replied that his shade would very
likely be gratified to find that my grandson
inherited my tastes in this respect. He then
picked up my book and remarked with surprise that in several chance met phrases this
despised writer had anticipated passages of
his own.

What really matters is that we shall not,
from enthusiasm for our own rediscoveries or
sheer reaction from popular neglect, fall into
the error of disproportionate praise. Every
age has its own points of contact not only with

the acknowledged classics but with those who may be deemed just to have failed to attain that rank. Indeed, he is a bold man who ventures to say where exactly the line is to be drawn between the two classes. In one of his essays Arnold names among the really great English poets, less than a score all told, Campbell and Moore. Contemporary opinion would not with anything approaching unanimity place these two higher than the subjects of some of my essays. And as none of the writers named herein has been judged worthy of inclusion in the series of 'English Men of Letters,' they may with propriety be classed as *Proxime Accessit*.

JOHN GOWER.

§ 1.

In the north aisle of the nave of the Cathedral church of St. Saviour, Southwark, on the spot where the chapel of St. John the Baptist is supposed formerly to have stood, is the tomb of John Gower. On the top of it is set the recumbent image of the dead poet, straight and stiff, stretched to his full length, his straight hair bound with a fillet, his face long and austere, his body clothed in a long black cassock, buttoned from the neck to the tip of his down-turned toes, over which the robe is decorously drawn. Round his neck is a collar of SS., and under his head, an honourable but hard pillow, his three books, with their names clearly inscribed—*Vox Clamantis* (the topmost), *Speculum Meditantis, Confessio Amantis.*

It would be hard to devise an image more emblematic of austerity, of dignified, decorous, cultured morality. Gower has not the air of a monk.   The man who lies there, you would say, was an ascetic but not a recluse; a puritan but not a fanatic; conservative but not a bigot.   Also, you might say, a scholar but not a poet.   There the thin nose and compressed lips would, I think, mislead you. Could you but see the eyes, which are decently hidden beneath the down-drawn lids, I think they would belie the mask of his other features. In any case the physiognomy of this statue cannot teach us a very great deal, for Stowe makes it clear that the features had already by his day been considerably 'restored'. But we cannot wonder at the epithet Chaucer, who knew him well, has attached to his name, 'O moral Gower'.

§ 2.

Concerning John Gower's life we have but scanty and uncertain knowledge.   Our chief authority is his writings, which, besides the indirect evidence a work of art always yields, in a greater or less degree, as to its maker, contain a few direct personal references. There is also his tomb.   Beyond these two sources of knowledge we have only the occurrence of the name or signature 'John Gower' in a few documents, which may, in a few instances probably, and in a few more possibly, be identified as that of the poet.

Early biographers, such as Leland, made such identifications in the wildest fashion and declared Gower to be possessed of land all over Kent and East Anglia. In one of the more likely cases, which is accepted by Sir Harris Nicolas, one John Gower is said to have received ' the manor of Aldyngton with a rent of 14s.6d., a cock, thirteen hens and a 140 eggs from Maplecomb.' But the obtaining of this manor seems to have been attended by such shady practices that Mr. Macaulay, who in the fourth volume of his edition of Gower's works has collected all the available information, refuses to admit the identification.

It seems certain, however, that the poet was a man of means and held lands in Kent. He may also have held others in Northampton, Norfolk and Suffolk. It may have been he who, by license dated 25 January, 1397, married one Agnes Groundolf. It is certainly he who, by a will dated 15 August 1408, and proved 24 October, 1408, bequeathed monies to certain Southwark churches, and rents in Northampton and Suffolk to his wife. He was living at the time of his death

1*

in the priory of St. Mary Overies, afterward
St. Saviour's, which foundation it is probable
he had already benefited during his life. It
has been alleged, as the result of one of the
identifications referred to, that the poet was
in holy orders, but this is incompatible with
his marriage.

We gather little of real moment from all
this except that he was a landed proprietor,
who lived an apparently uneventful and
pious life;   that he wrote *Speculum meditantis, Vox Clamantis* (in 1387), *Confessio
Amantis* at the request of Richard II, the
poet being then something over forty ; that
he was blind by the second year of Henry
IV's reign and died in the early autumn of
1408.   Also that he was at least acquainted
with the game of tennis.*

But the most famous thing about Gower
today is that he was a friend of Geoffrey
Chaucer.

§ 3.

No writer so dominates his age and country
as Chaucer does.   We think of that ' merrie '

---

* Of the Tenetz to winne or lese a chace
Mai no lif wite er that the bal be ronne.

In Praise of Peace, I. 295.

England of the fourteenth century as 'Chaucer's England,' of the tongue spoken by the people as 'Chaucer's English.' Even Wyclif's fame pales beside his, and the speech of some four parts of the nation lapses into 'dialect' mainly because it is not his. What chance has Gower, 'moral' Gower, of shining with more than a reflected lustre?

Chaucer and Gower were friends and in some respects friendly rivals. Each alludes to the other in his extant poetry. Chaucer jests in his sly way at his sober fellow poet: Gower incurs suspicion of not being able to take a joke well. But gentle Elia and excellent Bob Southey quarrelled worse than Chaucer and Gower can be said to have done. The reference to Gower by Chaucer, and, as quoted by writers on Chaucer, those the reverse way, are probably the best known things about the old poet today and they may at once be disposed of.

Chaucer, in the dedication of *Troilus and Cressida*, addresses his friends Gower and Strode :

> O morall Gower, this book I direct
> To thee and the philosophicall Strode,
> To vouchen safe there need is to correct
> Of your benignites and zeles good.

We know, too, that when Chaucer was sent to Lombardy with Sir Edward Berkely's mission, he appointed Gower one of two attorneys to act for him during his absence.

On the other part, at the end of the *Confessio Amantis,* in the first recension only, occurs the following reference to Chaucer:

> And gret wel Chaucer, whan ye mete,
> As mi disciple and mi poete.

The reason, it has been suggested, why this passage is missing in later M. SS. is that the two poets had quarrelled, and the alleged cause of this quarrel is Chaucer's strictures on the tales of Canace and of Apollonius of Tyre said to be implied in the Man of Lawe's words:

> "Of swiche cursed stories I say 'fy'."

There is, however, no necessity to presume any such quarrel. A more plausible explanation of the omission is that Chaucer was dead when the later version was made and so beyond the reach of his friend's embassage.

But even if they had had no personal intercourse the collocation of the two poets would be inevitable. In age they were very close. The birth of neither is exactly known, but probably Gower was born about 1325, Chau-

cer about 1340. Both passed their lives in
London and Kent, received roughly similar
educations and moved in the same circles,
though Gower was more of a scholar and
country gentleman, Chaucer more of a courtier and public official. Both were well acquainted with the literature, French, Latin
and Italian, current in that age, and they
used, roughly, the same sources. Both were
in the main tellers of tales and not lyric
poets. Both were, in politics and religion,
essentially moderate men, deploring the
time's abuses and favourable to reform, but
conservatives and disposed to support the
de facto government. Yet in their tempera-
ment and in their artistic method they are
strikingly different.

Chaucer seems naturally to associate himself with the spring, particularly with the
month of May. The Canterbury Pilgrims
rode forth on their immortal journey in
' Aprille '; but in a score of passages he cele-
brates the beauty of the succeeding month.
It is in May that Emilia's beauty strikes the
heart of Palamon and of Arcite, in May,
mother of glad months, that Troilus woos
fair Cressida.

And the whole mind and art of Chaucer are
consonant with this predilection. His world
is in its flowering time. His poetry is of the
renaissance, creating a new literature in his
native tongue, acclaiming the beauty of
youth and youthful virtues, of love and
loyalty to ideals. His very cynicism is the
clever, witty cynicism of youth. His England
is full of jingling bells and laughter on the
high road, of loaded boards and love talk
within doors. He is not without pity, nor
need we suppose him without vision of the
poverty and distress that lay at his door in
those days of the Black Death and the Peasant's Revolt. But these things are not his
trade. He sees beauty in the world, and
hope, and love; and in these and not in the
moral or physical epidemics of the time he
finds the eternal themes of poetry. And how
could he help the weary and distressed better
than by revealing to them that the sources
of joy could be found wherever there was
humanity, in any rank, to be studied, or
English fields in summer time to be looked
on?

When Chaucer points a moral, as he frequently does, he does it playfully and because
it emphasizes some detail in his story. When,

for example, the *auctor* intervenes in the
Clerk's Tale and reviles the fickleness of the
mob, it is to emphasize the completeness of
Griselda's fall from favour and all human
consolation, and thereby to stress her Job-
like patience, not from any desire to preach
to his fellow sinners. When, again, in the
Squire's Tale, he accuses the mob of ascrib-
ing always the baser of two possible motives,
he is evoking in his readers' minds a true
picture of an assemblage of village gossips.
We may be sure Chaucer did despise the
mob, but he would never have troubled to
tell us so if it had not been relevant to his
composition.

Very different is Gower. He had less
capacity for enjoyment, and less devotion to
beauty and to the comeliness and proportion
of his work. In other words, he is less of a
poet. Also he was more of a moralist. Many
of his tales are told badly and with no art,
they are merely so many additional lashes
upon the prostrate body of one of the Deadly
Sins. There is much, very much of the poet
in him, but the moralist is for ever cropping
up. He seems at times to forget all else in
the sheer joy of telling a good story well.
Then his hair shirt chafes him and he will

begin to reel off horrible examples of the
wages of sin, or make the scheme of his poetic
allegory ridiculous by such passages as the
denunciation of Paganism, and particularly
of the worship of Venus, proceeding from the
mouth of her own priest.

Gower, too, says much in praise of May,
such phrases are almost common-places in
mediaeval literature; but he is not filled, as
Chaucer is, with the very breath of the
month:

> Whan every bird hath chose his mate
> And thenketh his merthes for to make
> Of love, that he hath acheved.

We feel rather, in reading the *Confessio
Amantis,* that Gower is an autumnal poet,
and that in more ways than one. This may
be because this poem, his only long extant
piece in English, is the work of his latter
days, but it may be doubted if Gower was
ever as young as Chaucer was when, in
mature life, he wrote *The Canterbury Tales.*
Gower is an austere person, and we easily
associate him with that long, straight, black
recumbent statue of him on his tomb in St.
Saviour's. A very skilful writer he was, as a
metrist almost Chaucer's equal, writing a
long poem of some 30,000 lines, in uniform

metre throughout, and that in short lined couplets, most easy to render monotonous, with spirit, variety and unfailing smooth-ness.

Yet even in the best of the tales that make up this book we miss that supreme quality which Chaucer has; not by reason of Gower's inferior technique, for, though he has lapses, individual tales are as artistically presented as any except the very best of Chaucer's, but from the lack of that one greatest of gifts, a strong, living and attract-ive personality. Chaucer, even when he is directly adapting Boccaccio, is always per-sonal, vivid, creative; Gower, even when he departs furthest from his source, seems always to be writing in a vein which is deriv-ed from his authorities and his environment. His morals are the result of sound teaching ; his knowledge and his literary method, of wide reading and correct judgment.

Chaucer is of May, too, in looking forward. He is, a little prematurely, the first of our moderns, the founder of a great vernacular literature, a true peer of Wyclif in rejecting authority as the sole guide, antiquity as the sole source of knowledge, the old masters as the only models. He uses the old bottles, but he pours in new wine, and he makes new bottles of his own as well. In *Troilus and Cressida,* though in the main Boccaccio's, we have touches of psychology and a subtlety of manner which seem to forerun the comedy of Congreve, and in *The Canterbury Tales,* for all their romantic gear, we discern the mental attitude of a Fielding.

How different is Gower, who should have been the last of the Mediaevalists, had the fifteenth century been capable of profiting by Chaucer's unformulated teaching. Chaucer uses the allegory, skilfully but lightheartedly, and finally discards it ; Gower builds an enormous allegoric structure (of the precise, moral type, not the later romantic variety best known to us in Spenser) according to the approved mediaeval fashion, and much admirable detail is well-nigh lost in this ill-lit, ill-designed edifice.

§ 4.

The plan of the *Confessio Amantis* gives no chance to the poem as a whole. The theme is love, but love regarded in a formal, pedantic manner peculiar to the literary circles of the middle ages.

The poet introduces his collection of tales by relating how, being filled by the month of May with a yearning for love, he prayed to Cupid and to Venus for grace. Cupid thereupon threw a dart at him, but Venus enquired into the state of his heart and bad him go and be shriven by her priest. The priest proceeds to consider love in its relation to the Seven Deadly Sins, and examines the stricken poet on these several heads. On the one hand the priest relates stories illustrating the various errors into which lovers may fall, on the other the poet confesses his own state (which is seldom very sinful). ' My lady ' remains throughout a very vague and mythical person, and it is not clear whether ' she ' is in every case the same. There are, indeed, touches of naturalness in his relation of his failure to shine in her presence, but Chaucer, even in *The Legend of Good Women* or *The House of Fame,* could put more life into his allegoric frame than ever Gower could.

Gower goes on to work out his subdivision of the Art of Love in the mechanical, arithmetical fashion to which the mediaeval mind was so prone. The Seven Deadly Sins are considered under their several parts and a

summary, as thus: Pride—Hypocrisy, Inobed-
ience, Surquederie, Boasting, Vainglory,
Summary. Envy—Grudging, Gladness at
Others' Grief, Detraction, Dissimulation,
Supplantation, Summary. And so with the
rest. As a rule there is only one tale to illustrate each subdivision of a sin, but some
furnish more. Supplantation, for example,
is represented by the stories of Agamemnon
and Briseis, of Cressida and Diomede, of Am-
phitryon and Alcmene, of the False Bachelor
and the Caliph's Daughter, of Pope Boniface
and Pope Celestine, of Abner and Achitophel.
In length the stories vary from a mere
mention in a single line to the romance of
Apollonius of Tyre in nearly 2000 lines. But
this occurs in the last book, the 8th, and by
that time the symmetrical scheme of the
poem has been broken. Six books treat of six
of the Deadly Sins; book VII proceeds, from
a reference to the training of Alexander at
the end of book VI, to enlarge on that favourite theme of the mediaeval maker of books,
the Duties and Training of a King, and, since
Aristotle was Alexander's tutor, a long in-
accurate account of the sciences as known to
Aristotle is inserted. The four qualities first
set forth as necessary in governance are

Truth, Largesse, Pity, and Righteousness.
To these he adds the avoidance of the
hitherto unconsidered seventh Sin, which is,
however, more or less implicit in all the other
six when treated in relation to Love, to wit
Unchastity, and he can therefore claim to
have completed his programme. The eighth
book then professes to gather up 'oght over-
ronne, or oght foryete or left behinde', and
gives us a rapid outline of the book of Genesis, with some examples of incest, from
which point he launches forth into the story
of Apollonius.

Finally the poet is absolved by the priest,
whereupon he indites a poetical epistle to
Cupid and Venus, of which some verses are
as charming as anything in the poetry of the
age, and make us regret the loss of Gower's
earlier and lighter work, such as must have
gone to the making of so skilled a metrist.
Venus, in answer to this 'supplication',
appears, and the poet is granted a vision of
the great lovers of legend and romance:

> Ther was Tristram, which was beleved
> With bele Ysolde, and Lancelot
> Stod with Gunnore and Galahot*

---

* There is no man so chaste as to escape slander!
Who was this lady? Surely Malory, had he lived a

With his ladi, and as me thoghte
I syh where Jason with him broghte
His love, which Creusa hihte.

And so on for two hundred lines, wherein
the very names ring with the music of old re-
membrances. Then Cupid plucks forth his
dart, and the poet is declared free from all
further service in the court of Love. Here
occurs, or here is omitted, the reference already quoted to Chaucer, and the poem then
ends with a prayer for the good governance
of England, a prayer several times rewritten
to accord with the revolutions of the day.

To read the poem through as a whole from
end to end is not the way to get the most
pleasure from it. The parts are indubitably
greater than the whole. The whole is dull;
the parts, taken singly, are as a rule entertaining. Many of the world's greatest tales
appear in Gower's pages, and he tells them
worthily. He draws on the usual sources—
Ovid and the other Romans, *The Golden
Legend,* the Troy legends, in Guido de Col-
onna's or Benoit de St. Maure's collection,
Vincent of Beauvais' *Speculum Historiale,*
and a many more. As a rule he follows his

century earlier than he did, would have broken a lance
with Gower for such a statement.

original, but he does not hesitate to depart from it on occasions, and not without artistic success. He seems to have been very catholic in his taste, and so little scrupulous that his friend Chaucer, as we have seen, humorously makes his Man of Law protest against the lewdness of certain of his tales.

His stories are not all told with equal skill nor do they seem equally to suit his style. As a rule, the classical tales appear to less advantage than those of a more Gothic cast. The former need to be more formally and delicately beautiful; call, perhaps, for a more fluent and gracious language than the yet raw and ill-articulated English tongue. Moreover Gower, in spite of his moral bluntness in some respects, is always too austere and heavy-handed to do complete justice to the golden beauty of an Hellenic myth. Yet some even among these are admirable. The story of Rosiphele, of Protesilaus and of Alceon in book IV, of Deianira in book II, are good examples. Particularly well suited to Gower's style is such a gruesome story as that of Tereus in Book V, in which he improves on Ovid, being less bloody and introducing a pretty piece of fancy in the symbolism of the

2

nightingale and the swallow.* For Gower,
though he does here show commendable moderation, takes a most barbaric joy in blood
and horror, insisting, for example, twice over
on the outrage of Orestes on his mother's
corpse.

But the later stories suit his style better.
Here he evokes an image like a Dureresque
woodcut, and he is both powerful and original. An admirably told story is that of *The
Trump of Death* in Book I. Vigorous is the
scorn with which the king reproves his
brother who had despised his own humility:

> 'Ha, fol, how thou art for to wite,
> The king unto his brother seth,
> 'That thou art of so litel feith,
> That only for a trompes soun
> Hath gone dispuiled through the town
> Thou and thy wife in such manere
> Forth with thy children that ben here
> In sight of alle men aboute
> For that thou seist thou art in doute
> Of deth which stant under the lawe
> Of man, and man it mai withdrawe

---

* A like improvement on Ovid is in the story of
Leucothoe, the lover of the sun-god. In the *Metamor-
phoses* she is turned by Venus into a mere 'pot of
basil'. Gower more kindly represents her as a sun-
flower ever 'following her sun':

> 'Sche sprong up out of the molde
> Into a flour, was named golde
> Which stant governed of the Sonne.'

So that it mai per chance faile,
Now schalt thou noght forthy mervaile
That I doun fro my charr alihte
Whanne I beheld to-fore my sihte
In hem that were of so gret age
Min oghne deth thurgh here ymage,
Which God hath set be lawe of kinde,
Whereof I mai no bote finde.

.   .   .   .

The story of the Loathly Bride is admirably told, sustaining even the inevitable comparison with Chaucer's rendering of the same tale, put into the mouth of the immortal Wife of Bath. But in *The Canterbury Tales* the story is almost 'distained' by its own prologue, which, moreover, colours it with its humour. Gower's version differs in several points. He gives the knight's name, Florent, and omits all reference to King Arthur. He makes Florent promise, before the lady will tell him the answer to the enigma, and that after much haggling, that he will wed her. In Chaucer, the knight easily promises to grant whatever his informant may hereafter ask, and she subsequently appears before the Queen and claims him. Gower's version, making it more of a cash transaction, is less in the romantic manner but more convincing. Gower, with an eye to the practical, dwells

on the difficulty of making the hag look like
a bride :

> She hadde bath, she hadde reste
> And was arraied to the beste.
> But with no craft of combes brode
> Thei myhte her hore lockes schode.
>
> . . . .
>
> Bot whan sche was fulliche arraied
> And her atyr was al assaied,
> Tho was sche fouler on to se.

When the marriage comes to be consum-
mated, Florent takes the plunge like a man
who after long hesitation enters cold water.
Then,

> He torneth him al sodeinly
> And syh a lady lay him by
> Of eyhtetiene wynter age
> Which was the faireste of visage,
> That evere in all this world he syh.

In Chaucer, the wedded and bedded pair
hold a long parley, discussing the nice ethical problem: Is it better to have a foul but
faithful wife, or one loose and lovely? It
must, of course, be remembered that it is not
Geoffrey Chaucer who is telling this tale,
but the Wife of Bath.

§ 5.

As a metrist Gower is remarkable. Before
he came to write his long English poem he

had, we may be sure, written plenty of short
ones, though they have not survived ; a loss
similar to that which is to be deplored in Chaucer's case. Also he had train-
ed his facility in the writing of great
lengths of fluent yet varied verse by composition of a long Latin and a long
French poem. From the latter tongue
in particular he would have learned, as did
Wyatt in one later age and Waller in another,
to be smooth and prosodically ' correct '. It
is indeed little short of a miracle how easily
and sweetly Gower makes his rather stiff
and angular language flow. Compared with
the crudities of his predecessors, or even with
the monotonous jog-trot of his contemporary,
Barbour, he is Hyperion to a Satyr. Chaucer
himself is not a more accomplished crafts-
man, and his immediate successors, Lydgate
and Occleve, cannot even profit by his
example. Except for the closing invocation
the whole of the *Confessio Amantis* is in
octo-syllabic couplets, to which he imparts
frequent and apt modifications of rhythm.
He uses most skilfully such repetitions as
' He waiteth time, he waiteth place ', or

> Torne it to wo, torne it to wele,
> Torne it to good, torne it to harm.

which break effectively the fluent lines, with level stresses in the French mode, which make up the mass of his verse. He can quicken his rhythm, too, with such lines as

> The night was dark, there shone no mone,
> To-fore the gates he came sone.

He shows something of Spenser's art in his description of the House of Sleep:

> Under an hell ther is a cave
> Which of the sonne mai noght have,
> So that no man may knowe ariht
> The point between the dai and nyht,
> There is no fyr, ther is no sparke,
> There is no dore which mai charke,
> Wherof an yhe scholde unschette,
> So that inward ther is no lette.
> And for to speke of that withoute
> Ther stant no gret tre nyh aboute
> Wheron there myhte crowe or pie
> Alihte for to clepe or crie.
> Ther is no cok to crowe day,
> Ne beste none which noise may,
> The hell, bot al aboute round
> Ther is growende upon the ground
> Popi, which berith the sed of slep,
> With othre herbes such an hep,
> A stille water for the nones
> Rennende upon the smale stones
> Which hihte of Lethes the rivere,
> Under that hell in such manere
> Ther is, which yifth great appetit
> To slepe. And thus full of delit
> Slep hath his hous, and of his couche
> Withinne his chambre if I schal touche
> Of hebenus that slepi tree

> The bordes al aboute be,
> And for he scholde slepe softe
> Upon a fethrebed alofte
> He lith with many a pilwe of doun.

Read with the proper distribution of stress, with a broad pronunciation of the vowels and due observance of the now mute e, where not elided, no verse can be more satisfying to the tongue or to the ear.

Here is yet one more sample of Gower's skill, from the story of Rosiphele:

> Sche sih the swote floures springe,
> Sche herde glade foules singe.
> Sche sih the bestes in her kinde
> The buck, the do, the hert, the hinde,
> The male go with the female
> And so began there a querele
> Between love and her oghne herte
> Fro which sche couthe noght asterte.

Nor was his skill limited to this one metre. The 'supplication', in stanzas of seven decasyllabic lines, is equally polished.

> Upon miself if thilke tale come
> Hou whilom Pan, which is the god of kinde,
> With Love wrastlede and was overcome ;
> For ever I wrastle and evere I am behinde,
> That I no strengthe in al min herte finde
> Whereof that I mai stonden eny throwe ;
> So fer mi wit with love is overthrowe.

That is almost Jacobean in its mellow harmony. Still better, perhaps, are some parts of the short poem called *In Praise of Peace*,

one of the very few of Gower's shorter
pieces to survive. Such a line as

For vein honour or for the worldes good

has the authentic ring of the 'mighty line'

§ 6.

Humour is not Gower's strong point.
Indeed it is notably lacking to the reader
new-come to his pages from those of Chaucer, who can hardly refrain from revealing
the comic lining to his most tragic clouds.
But he employs at times a certain wittiness
of phrase, and even displays humour of a
pawky type which gains in effectiveness
from its rarity.

He seide, nay. Thei seiden, yis.
The lettre shewed, rad it is,
Which thei forsoken everidel

There is a vivacity of manner in such lines
as these which contributes its share to the
freshness of the long poem. His jesting reference to Aristotle in the vision of lovers
shows that Gower was no mirthless pedant:

I syh there Aristotle also
Whom that the queene of Grece so
Hath bridled, that in thilke time
Sche made him such a silogime
That he foryat al his logique.

Pleasant too are the pithy saws and popular sayings which he frequently introduces into his polished verse. The appearance of their familiar faces is continually giving the reader a pleasant surprise—'between two stoles is the fall,' 'Lo, how thei feignen chalk for chese', 'And as a cat wolde ete fishes, Withoute wetinge of his cles.'

In yet another vein he achieves a witty, satiric epigram in the course of a dissertation, by the priest, on Avarice (*C. A.,* Book V) :

> Whil that a man hath good to yive
> With grete routes he mai live
> And hath his frendes overal
> And everich of him telle shal.
> Therwhile he hath his fulle packe,
> They say, 'A good felawe is Jacke'.
> But whanne it faileth atte last,
> Anone his pris thei overcaste.
> For thanne is ther non other lawe
> But 'Jacke was a good felawe'.

§ 7.

It would not be fair to Gower's memory to leave him without paying a tribute to the love of his country which he shows in every part of his work. His substitution of Henry for Richard as the addressee of the *Confessio Amantis* has exposed him to the charge of being a turncoat. This, however, is quite undeserved. Gower was no politician. He hated all extremes and all illegalities, denouncing alike the rich who oppress the poor and the poor who rob and murder the rich. In his attitude towards the reformers of the age he is at one with the author of *Piers Plowman* and Wyclif, but he sternly rebukes the Lollards, to whom his attitude is not unlike that of Wordsworth towards the Revolutionaries. He shrinks appalled from the means by which it is sought to bring about desirable ends. To Richard as King of England he appeals, urging him to act for the country's welfare. But Richard had disappointed his early hopes and had shown that he lacked the first essential in the head of a government, the power to keep internal order. When Henry comes to the fore, Gower appeals to him with the same end in view. Dynasties mattered little, the welfare of the country mattered much. There is nothing to show that he was ever a partisan of Richard as against Henry, or was under any personal obligation to him.

It is in especial for peace and unity that Gower ever prays, and that the King will remember that

Ther may non erthly kyng suffise
Of his kyngdom the folk to lede,
Bot he the Kyng of Hevene drede,

in the beautiful poem *In Praise of Peace,* the most eloquent expression of Gower's sincere and wise patriotism. The same theme inspires his long Latin poem, *Vox Clamantis,* which is one long outpouring of the poet's grief over the moral decay of his well loved England.

§ 8.

This poem and the French *Miroir* are not likely to find many readers, and little need be said of them. The French poem was the earliest of the three, and for a long while was known only from its use as the poet's pillow on his tomb and from a reference at the close of the *Vox Clamantis.* In both places it is spoken of as *Speculum Meditantis.* Recently, however, Mr. Macaulay discovered a M. S. in the Cambridge University library. Here it is entitled *Le Miroui de l'Omme.* The theme of the poem is marriage, and though it has been praised for the correctness of its French and of its prosody, it is the least interesting as well as the shortest of the three long poems. It is a formal, artificial piece, thoroughly mediaeval in its conception and dull in its execution.

The Latin poem, *Vox Clamantis,* is a more interesting and personal utterance. Here, too, in the current fashion, the poet fabricates a dream, in which he undergoes sundry allegorical adventures. Men in the fields are turned into beasts, and one terrible Boar ranges through Kent and another comes from the north. The poet flees to a ship and there is tossed in a great storm. Then one William, a mayor, strikes down one of the monsters and the storm subsides. The events symbolized by all this—the Peasants' revolt, the siege of the Tower, and the death of Wat Tyler—are easy to recognize. Gower then proceeds to examine the causes of the present discontents, and arraigns the three degrees of society—clergy, knights, and peasantry—for their respective vices. He concludes with an appeal to the king as the power from which in the last resort all good must flow.

Of the earnest patriotism of the poem I have already spoken. The Latinity is good, judged by the standard of the age, but the elegiac couplet lacks here the grace and sweetness of the true Roman style. It abounds, however, in those ingenuities to

which the metre has ever lent itself.   It is
thus, for instance, that the poet proclaims
his name :

> Primos sume pedes Godefridi, desque Johanni
> Principiumque sui Wallia jungat eis :
> Ter caput amittens det cetera membra, que tali
> Carmine compositi nominis ordo patet.

And thus the date of the composition :

> Tolle caput mundi, C ter et sex lustra fer illi,
> Et decies quinque cum septem post super adde:
> Tempus tale nota, qui tunc fuit Anglia mota.

§ 9.

There is perhaps nothing of the highest
poetry in Gower. He does not make us see
visions, or feel more intensely any of the
great emotions of human life. He does not
light up the dark places of man's soul, laying
bare motives or analysing thoughts. He tells
his stories plainly or prettily, wisely and, at
times, wittily, turning aside not at all to elaborate the character of any of his personages
or theorize on the why and the wherefore.
The priest points out the moral bearing of
the tales, but in general terms and with no
enhancement of the value of the stories as
works of art. Gower is thoroughly mediaeval
in his method of proving his general laws by
a simple enumeration of instances, piling

instance upon instance with very little niceness of discrimination.

Yet Gower is a true poet. He feels for and with the personages of his tales, and by his choice of words conveys to us not the bare facts only, but something of the atmosphere in which his imagination sees them happen, something, too, of his own feelings of pity or scorn. The tales would not, to meet the obvious criticism, be equally well told in prose. A prose version of the stories is certainly possible and does in many cases exist; but the reader of prose demands a more exact story and a greater verisimilitude. The melody and ingenuity of verse rightly disarm criticism in this respect; they enable the mind to acquiesce in certain conventions in which it is very pleasant to acquiesce. Prose is the language of reason, and when addressed in it we are all of the family of Didymus. The prose romancer has indeed his own way of overcoming our doubts, or of evading them. But the poet's way is the older and better way. He does not give the Cerberus of our logical mind a cake, that looks like the real thing but is not. Like Orpheus he wins his way by the power of melody.

SIR THOMAS NORTH.

§ 1.

IT IS a curious fact that though most persons with any literary knowledge associate Plutarch in English with the name of Thomas North, yet other, later translations have for two centuries and more had a much wider vogue. There is one popular reprint of North to half-a-dozen of his rivals, and the old book-shops will almost always yield an eighteenth century Langhorne, or a socalled Dryden (of which version the best known nineteenth century edition, Clough's, is a revision).

But it was in North's magnificent prose that Englishmen from the days of Shakespeare and Raleigh to the days of Milton and Marlborough read that great and unrivalled collection of the life stories of heroes, and learned from their examples to make life a high adventure and to spend themselves in the service of the community.

For this surely is Plutarch's glory, not
that he was a great historian tracing the
progress of a nation or of an institution, but
the celebrant of great deeds and great men,
giving us by anecdote and pithy analysis the
characters and motives, the very form and
pressure of the Hero. And Plutarch's heroes
are so full of warmth and spirit, so human
and so gallant, that the reader of generous
blood is fired to emulation and resolves to
serve England with no less love and endur-
ance than Themistocles served Athens, or
Coriolanus Rome; to pursue fame no less
eagerly than Alexander; to preserve honour
and justice no less firmly than Numa Pompi-
lius. It is for this combination of true virtue
with Renaissance *vertu,* or godliness with
manliness, a kind of *splendid morality,* that
Plutarch's pages are to be prized, and it was
for this that North, an Elizabethan of the
finest type, serving Gloriana (who is England rather than Elizabeth) no less with his
pen than he was ever ready to serve her with
his sword, rendered the *Lives* into his native
tongue. And this achievement, the central
one of his life, was typical of all the rest
of it.

§ 2.

Thomas North was one of that most estimable of English breeds, the country gentlemen, and one who remained all his life unusually true to type. His father had been raised to the peerage, but to Thomas, as a younger son, that made little difference. He went to court, but only, it would seem, to display his loyalty; he never held any kind of post there and seems to have been unambitious of court advancement. But we have very few details of his life, and a great deal of what might pass for his biography (which has never been written at any length) would have to be conjectural.

He was born about the year 1535, the son of Sir Edward North of Kirthling. Of his education nothing is known, but it is thought that he may have been entered at Peterhouse, Cambridge, of which foundation his father had been a benefactor. The first certain fact about him is that in 1557 we find him in London, residing in Lincoln's Inn, of which he was a member. From here, at the age of 22 or thereabouts, he dated his first book, *The Diall of Princes,* an English version, through the French, of the Spanish

Lo Relox de Principes by Antonio de Guevara, a book of anecdotes and moral disquisi-
tions for the edification of princes. His
object in translating it almost certainly was
not a mere desire for literary fame, nor yet
zeal for pure learning. The motive of North's
life was, as was typical of his class and age,
patriotism. He sincerely hoped to help his
country to good government by translating
this already famous book, which he loyally
dedicated to Queen Mary.

His second undertaking was of a similar
nature. It also was a translation, and of a
work of a moral character pertaining to the
science of government, albeit North was too
well acquainted with the tastes of his own
kind to choose a book that lacked a notable
attractiveness in its lighter elements. This
second work was *The Morall Philosophie of
Doni,* a rendering of the Florentine version
of the *Fables of Bidpai,* one of the oldest
collections of beast-tales in the world. This
appeared in 1570.

While still quite young North had married
Elizabeth, daughter of Jeffrey Colvile, of
Newton in the Isle of Ely. Two children,
Edward and Elizabeth, are mentioned in the
will of his father, Edward, 1st Lord North.

which is dated 20 March, 1563. Thus Thomas,
true to his character of country gentleman,
married a neighbour (though Jeffrey Colvile is described in this connection as of
London and owned property in Kent as well
as in Cambridgeshire), and his two children
here mentioned also married in the neighbourhood, Edward marrying one Elizabeth
Wren, of Haddenham, in the Isle; Elizabeth,
Thomas Stuteville, of Brinkley in Cambridgeshire. North's own second wife was
Judith Vesey, of Isleham, also in Cambridgeshire. These genealogical details are interesting as suggesting a marked homekeep-
ing instinct in Thomas North's strain.

He must himself by this time have established a personal connection with Cambridgeshire, for in 1568 he was granted the
freedom of the City of Cambridge. Nevertheless in 1574 he accompanied his brother
Roger, now the 2nd Lord North, to France
on state business; and here, it is likely, he
met one whose influence decided the exact
nature of his after-fame, Jaques Amyot, Bishop of Auxerre. Five years later he published his translation, after Amyot's French, of
Plutarch's *Lives*. With this, strange to say,
his publications end (except for a few ad-

ditions and a new dedication to the third edition of Plutarch), though his public activities are far from doing so. Plainly it was no *cacoethes scribendi* that urged Thomas North into authorship. He was never either a professed scholar or a man of letters. He was throughout his life a country gentleman, serving the Queen's Majesty in the capacity that best became him, with pen or sword, in the field or on the bench. In the Armada year he assumed command of 300 men of Ely, and he was knighted in 1591. I should like also to believe that he is the Sir Thomas North who is stated in a M. S. preserved at Hatfield to have commanded a company of 100 men on service in Ireland during Tyrone's rebellion; though it does not need this last signal instance to make me sure that unassuming and unswerving devotion to his country was the guiding principle of North's life, alike in his literary labours and in practical affairs.

He is supposed to have died about the year 1601.

§ 3.

A closer examination of North's writings will confirm the impression of the civic purpose, that, together with a strong natural instinct for the art of writing prose, informs his work. At the same time it may be judged how remarkable was his skill in the choice of words and in their manipulation, and his sense of rhythm.

It may be remarked, first, that the dedications of his translated books are the only original compositions of North's we have. Though in the first class of prose-writers of his age, and displaying even in translation a strong and charming personality, North seems never to have attempted any direct expression of his views. He may have known his own limitations better than we do: he may have been over-diffident. His modesty is evident and honourable. In the presence of so many master minds, whose works had been acclaimed by all the peoples of Europe, how should the simple Cambridgeshire gentleman seek to air his own views, while these others were still unknown, or imperfectly known, to Englishmen?

The work to the translation of which he devoted his earliest labours was at that time one of the most celebrated and widely read books in the world. Guevara was a courtier of the Emperor Charles V, as well as a Bish-

op and a renowned preacher. In 1528 there
was printed at Seville a volume called *Libro
aureo de Marco Aurelio: emperador: y elo-
quentissimo orador*.   In the following year
there was printed at Valladolid the *Libro de
Marco Aurelio cō relox de principes,* the
author of which, it was added, is the Bishop
of Guadix. This second book is several times
longer than the first, the whole of which it
incorporates, and Guevara, at that time
Bishop of Guadix, asserted that the early
version was unauthorized and printed from
stolen copy. But the shorter book offered
obvious advantages to publishers and translators, and both versions therefore continued
to be current, not only in Spain but in all the
tongues of civilized Europe. In England the
Libro aureo found an illustrious translator
in Lord Berners, who, in the last years of his
life, translated it, through the French, under
the title of *The golden Book of Marcus Aurelius*.   This was published after Berners'
death, the first extant edition being dated
1535.   It was frequently reprinted, but the
longer, authorized version of the book was
never translated into English till North took
it in hand and published it under the title of
The Diall of Princes (Relox de principes) in

1557. To the three books here contained he added, in 1568, a fourth book entitled *The Favoured Courtier,* which is a translation of a later book of Guevara's, *Libro llamado aviso de privados,* not published in Spain till 1539.

The Diall, like *The Golden Book,* achieved wide popularity, and Guevara's other works also attained some vogue, finding translators in Geoffrey Fenton and Edward Hellowes.* Some modern critics regard this high popularity of Guevara, even in the dress provided for him by North, as a sign of the defective taste of the Elizabethan public. One wonders whether, when Elizabethan England and Georgian Fleet Street disagree, it may safely be assumed that it is necessarily the modern who is the superior. Those who like the rotund but perspicuous phrases of the best Tudor prose will enjoy *The Diall.* They will

---

* North himself, though possibly he did not know it, translated at the very end of his life another of Guevara's books. In 1567 an edition of Amyot's Plutarch was published containing a version by S. G. S. (Simon Goulard) of Guevara's *Una decada de las vidas de los X Emperadores romanos, desde Trajano a Alexandro,* a book translated by Hellowes as *A Chronicle, conteyning the lives of tenne Emperors of Rome,* (1577). These same Lives are added to the third edition (1603) of North's Plutarch.

know that it is idle to look in such a book
for a properly scaled and surveyed study of
any theme.   To the making of the mediaeval
book there was literally no end.   It was
bounded only by the extent of the author's
knowledge of the universe, and, further, by
the library he had at his command.   Almost
all books were compilations of older material,
most authors literary jackdaws of very ac-
quisitive tastes. Guevara's book has been described as a didactic novel, and as a version of
the *Meditations*. It is certainly didactic, as
practically all prose literature of those ages
was, but it is not in any sense a novel, and it
has no connection with the Meditations other
than the name of Marcus Aurelius, who is the
supposed author or recipient of the letters
and rhetorical effusions of which the book
consists.

The ground of its appeal to North is plain.
It is throughout a plea for moderation and
modesty, in politics and in behaviour ; even,
though Guevara was an Inquisitor, for tolera-
tion in religion.   Guevara is diffuse and
prolix, but he gives an impression of honesty
and breadth of mind, and sets forth the evils
of the misuse of power, which must recoil on
the head of its wielder, the need for orderly

government and of true religion, the nature
of education and of a mother's duty to her
children, of the importance of sobriety in
eating and in apparel, the blessings of peace,
the relations to be observed between the
sexes and between rich and poor, and a score
of such topics, all directed to the improvement of social conditions in the contemporary state, on the assumption that the Prince
was the fountain-head of all moral excellence
as well as of honour. To the serious-minded
young gentleman of the East Midlands (the
most enlightened part of England and the
most distressed by the accidents of the times)
in the days of the Marian troubles, the need
for such a sane, equable, moderate state of
mind as Guevara inculcates was very plain.
All North's writings were directed to this
same end.

To the reader the same qualities would
appeal. The reader of that day was, where
books were concerned, a serious person and
had not yet acquired that all-absorbing passion for the novel form which afflicts our own
generation. Yet he too liked a touch of the
personal element, the ' story ' quality so dear
to the modern journalist, when he could get
it. So allegory was the accepted mode of pre-

senting moral truths, and the incidental anecdotes, rather than the very loose threads of
the Emperor's biography, were the sugar that
helped the consumption of the moral medicine of *The Diall*. The modern reader finds
the book too heavy to read in bulk, but
his Elizabethan forebear was nurtured on
tougher stuff and thought this light and
pleasant fare, albeit wholesome and nourish-
ing; and since he had few books he did not
cavil at the great length (over 400,000 words)
of this one. So it came about that in all
languages the book was amazingly popular,
and the English reader of *The Diall* had in
addition the advantage of reading the prose
of a great master.

The terms of Mary's title alone would lend
distinction to any dedication:

> To the most high and virtuous princess Mary, by
> the Grace of God Queen of England, Spain, France,
> both Sicilies, Jerusalem, Naples, and Ireland, De-
> fender of the Faith, Archduchess of Austria, Duchess
> of Burgundy, Milan and Brabant, Countess of
> Hapsburg, Flanders and Tyrol, long health and
> perpetual felicity.

He goes on:

> The Divine Philosopher Plato, most gracious
> sovereign Lady, travailing all his life time to
> abolish the barbarous manners of the Grecians and
> to induce a civil form of living among the people,

ordained a law to the great comfort of those that
followed virtue and no less to the terror of others
that haunted vices. The which commanded, that not
only those which brought in or invented any new
thing that might either corrupt the good manners,
violate the ancient customs, hinder through evil
example the good living, empoison with erroneous
doctrine the consciences, effeminate with voluptuous
pleasures the heart, impoverish with unprofitable
merchandise the people or defame with malicious
words the renowns, should be (as unprofitable
members) from the common wealth expelled and
banished : but also ordained that those which
studied to publish any institution appertaining
either to the honour of the gods, to the reformation
of the frailty of men, or by any other means to the
profit of the weal public, should be condignly of
the common wealth entertained, preferred and
honoured.

On these grounds, he declares, Don Antony
of Guevara is highly to be praised, for all
his writings are to the glory of God and the
profit of His people, but most especially this
one, *Lo relox de principes,* for

there is no author (the sacred letters set apart) that
more effectually setteth out the omnipotency of
God, the frailty of men, the inconstancy of fortune,
the vanity of this world, the misery of this life,
and finally that more plainly teacheth the good
which mortal men ought to pursue and the evil
that all men ought to fly, than this present work
doth. The which is so full of high doctrine, so
adorned with ancient histories, so authorized with
grave sentences and so beautified with apt simili-
tudes, that I know not whose eyes in reading it
can be wearied, nor whose ears in hearing it not
satisfied.

This passage, particularly the last lines, shows North in his most rhetorical mood, as the occasion, a Royal dedication, requires. His style is not ordinarly so elaborate as this and the suggestion that it was to this book of his that all that kind of writing known as Euphuism is due is now generally regarded as going too far. The art of prose was just then being much studied, and North is already one of its masters ; but he was not alone even at this date in using rhetorical devices of various kinds, and Lyly, whose *Euphues* displays the highest contemporary level of ' conceited ' writing, might well have written as he did without any reference to *The Diall.* Doubtless he knew *The Diall :* probably every living writer did ; but it is only one among many exemplifications of a current fashion. North himself did not develop the ' conceited ' element in his own style. *The Favoured Courtier* of 1568 has less of it than the original three books of *The Diall,* and in his later works he is rather notably free from it.

§ 4.

The Diall is a translation through French of a Spanish original, and as some of the letters appended to it are stated not to be ' in the French copy ', North may be credited with some knowledge of the Spanish tongue. His second book gives further proof of linguistic skill, being a translation from an Italian version of the fables of Bidpai, a collection which experts in folk-lore trace back to Sanskritic and Pali originals more than a thousand years before Doni or North. The title of this book, which was printed in 1570, runs :

> The Morall Philosophie of Doni: Drawne out of the Auncient writers. A work first compiled in the Indian tongue, and afterwards reduced into divers other languages : and now lastly Englished out of Italian by Thomas North, Brother to the Right Honourable Sir Roger North Knight, Lorde North of Kyrtheling.

This is one of the most entertaining books of beast fables ever compiled, and North is justified in drawing attention, in his words 'To the Reader', to the sequence and cohesion of the stories :

> The stories, fables and tales, are very pleasant and compendious. Moreover the similitudes and comparisons doe (as they say) holde hands one with the other, they are so linked together . . . . . If you do not read in their proper order, you shall thinke them ryding tales spoken to no purpose, but to occupie your eares, and consume.

Which would seem to suggest that Thomas North did not greatly esteem *The Canter-*

bury Tales. But again it is the serious, civic purpose that inspires our translator. There is no dedication in this book, but in a set of verses ' to the reader ' he points out what he conceives to be its value to his countrymen. These verses are spirited enough to deserve quotation at length :*

T. N. TO THE READER.

Of wordes and of examples is a sundrie sort of speache,
One selfe same thing to minds of men in sundrie wise
        they teache :
Wordes teache but those that understande the language
        that they heare :
But things, to men of sundrie speache, examples make
        appeare.
So larger is the speache of beasts, though mens more
        certaine bee :
But yet so larger as conceyte is able them to see.
Such largenesse yet at length to bring to certaine use
        and plane,
God gave such grace to beasts that they should Indian
        speach attaine.
And then they learnde Italian tongue, and now at
        length they can,
By help of North, speake English well to every
        English man.
In English now they teache us wit. It English now
        they saye,
Ye men, come learne of beasts to live, to rule, and
        to obaye,

---

* These are the only original verses of North's I know. But the verse translations which occur in all his books are vigorous and good, much above the average in this kind.

To guide you wisely in the worlde, to know to shunne
        deceite,
To flie the crooked paths of guile, to keepe your
        doings straight.
As earst therefore you used beasts, but for your
        bodies neede,
Sometime to clothe, sometime to beare, sometime
        your selves to feede.
Now use them for behoofe of minde, and for your
        soules delite,
And wishe him well that taught them so to speake
        and so to write.

But *The Morall Philosophie,* in spite of its
grave title, is a very much lighter piece, as
well as a much shorter one, than *The Diall.*
It tells how the Mule, or Moyle in North's
spelling, slanders the noble Bull to King
Lion, and causes his death, in retribution for
which he is himself accused by the Libbard
and the Lioness, and, in spite of all his
'stamping and snuffing and flinging and
yerking' and 'taking on like a furie of
Hell', executed. But every move in the
game is punctuated by an illustrative story,
or string of stories, of the doings, as a rule,
of other beasts in like case. North uses
his clear and noble style with admirable
effect in this almost playful task. Consider,
for example, the witty gravity of such a
passage as this, descriptive of the Bull's re-
ception at the Lion's court:

The King bade him stande up, and willed him to tell the cause why he kept so long in those fields, and what hee ment to braye and rore so terribbly. The Bull tooke upon him the oratores part, and standing aside from the beginning to the ende he tolde him the whole discourse of his miseries . . . . The King wondering at his yeares, commanded streight stables should be provided for his Lordship, and gave him an infinite number of servaunts to wayte upon him, making him Prince of Bulles, Duke of Beefes, Marquesse of Calves, and Earle and Lorde great Maister of Kyne: and with a wonderful great provision he furnished hys rackes yearly, and made him of his privie counsell. After he had imployed him a while hee knewe his worthiness and discretion : so that in the ende he made him Viceroy and greatest Lorde of his Realme.

North here employs, too, a livelier and racier mode of conducting dialogue than the more serious, episcopal utterance of Guevara had admitted. The free use of vernacular words and phrases is an excellence of his as of all the best Tudor prose. Here is a passage from the edifying history ' of three great fishes :'

And the thirde was called of the Frogge ten times that hee shoulde rise and awake : whooe, but all in vayne.

He punched him for the nonste, and jogged hym agayne to make him awake, but it woulde not be. And he, tut, lyke a sluggarde, answered hym,

"I will ryse anone, anone : I pray thee let me alone a while, let me lye yet a little curtesie and then have with thee."

Stil the Fishers went on apace with their nets, and let go the water.

On the other hand he can describe a scene with a simple charm and easy rhythm that is far removed from the ornate and witty mode of Lyly or Sidney:

There dwelled a great Paragone of India (of those that live a hundreth yeares and never mue their feathers), a bird of the water, aire, and earth, in a great thicke close knot of Rosemaire uppon a pleasaunt Lake, placed beneath amongst the little hilles spred over with herbes and flowers. And always in his youth he lived (as his nature is) of fishe, the which with some devise he tooke by moon light with great sweat and labor.

Such writing may have involved North, as his prefatory note suggests, in ' travayle '; it certainly does not inflict on us ' painefull reading '.

This book is of extreme rarity. There appear to have been but two editions, one in 1570, the other in 1601; and Mr. Jacobs, who edited a reprint in 1888, could trace only a single complete copy of each. It would seem therefore as if it did not attain the popularity of North's other two productions, and being regarded as a ' slight, unmeritable ' piece, the copies that were current were not preserved with any care.

4

§ 5.

Our author's third and last work was in all respects his finest. It is the finest original, both in its matter and its manner, and North's own style here attains its full excellence.

Plutarch's Lives ... Englished by Sir Thomas North, appeared in 1579, with a dedication to Queen Elizabeth which again emphasizes the practical, moral purpose of the work :

> For among all the profane books, that are in reputation at this day, there is none (your Highness best knows) that teacheth so much honour, love, obedience, reverence, zeal and devotion to Princes, as these lives of Plutarch do. How many examples shall your subjects read here, of several persons and whole armies, of noble and base, of young and old, that both by sea and land, at home and abroad, have strained their wits, not regarded their states, ventured their persons, cast away their lives, not only for the honour and safety, but also for the pleasure of their Princes? *

The same note is sounded in his prefatory address ' To the Reader ', in which he further declares his love for Plutarch, the author of ' the profitablest story of all authors ', and refers his reader to Amyot's words, in the

---

* So Plutarch speaks of Solon as ' a perfect example and looking glass wherein men may see how to govern a popular state '.

like place, concerning 'the profit of stories'. Here Amyot insists on the teaching as well as the delight to be sought in books, and praises the writers of history above all others for making these two go arm in arm. 'History', he continues,

'is the very treasure of man's life, whereby the notable doings and sayings of men, and the wonderful adventures and strange cases (which the long continuance of time bringeth forth) are preserved from the death of forgetfulness ... there is neither picture, nor image of marble, nor arch of triumph, nor pillar, nor sumptuous sepulchre, that can match the durableness of an eloquent history ... it is a certain rule and instruction, which by examples past teacheth us to judge of things present, and to foresee things to come ... Likewise ... the immortal praise and glory wherewith it rewardeth well doers, is a very lively and sharp spur for men of noble courage and gentlemanlike nature, to cause them to adventure upon all manner of noble and great things. For books are full of examples of men of high courage and wisedom, who for desire to continue the remembrance of their name, by the sure and certain record of histories, have willingly yielded their lives to the service of the common weal, have spent their goods, sustained infinite pains both of body and mind in defence of the oppressed, in making common buildings, in stablishing of laws and governments, and in the finding out of arts and sciences necessary for the maintenance and ornament of man's life: for the faithful registring whereof, the thank is due to histories.'

In particular, asserts Amyot, and North would entirely agree with him, historians

are delightful and profitable to princes and
kings, who are otherwise most subject to
flattery and have least time for self-improve-
ment. In brief, North might regard the book
as another *Diall of Princes*.

But the present book is a far more valuable
gift to his countrymen than the earlier one.
The *Diall of Princes* was not, in its original,
one of the world's great masterpieces: Plutarch's *Lives* was. North's translation of *The
Diall* is a ' green and youthful ' production,
though skilful, interesting and distinguished
already for its style among the prose books
of a not very skilful age. Since 1557 English
prose had progressed. Lyly had outshone
North in sheer decorativeness, and the general level of narrative and expository prose
had wonderfully risen. A decade was now
reached which saw published the work of
Sidney, Bacon, Hooker, Raleigh and Shakespeare (a supremely great prose-writer), not
to mention a score of lesser men of an excellence in this art hardly known to the preced-
ing generation. But North had progressed
too, and could write with as much vigour and
pregnancy of phrase as the best of them. All
good Tudor prose has a freedom, a copious-
ness, a touch of splendour in its verbiage and

of athletic vigour in the handling of it hardly
to be matched in any other age. Much of its
richness is due to the youthfulness of the
language, which made possible an abandon
and an audacity not to be looked for in its
reasonable, sober, practised maturity. To
these qualities common to his generation
North adds very distinguished ones of his
own—the reflections of his personality—
simple directness, dignity, self-control, an
utter absence of pedantry, and a reverence
for the heroic which makes his pages ring
with the authentic accents of his heroes.

§ 6.

Plutarch's *Lives* is one of the world's
great books, but it is open to question
whether Plutarch is really one of the world's
great writers. He was born at Chaeronea in
about the year 50 B. C., a Greek provincial in
an age of Grecian decadence. He is not a
great stylist and though a most interesting
and alert-minded person not above the suspicion of being a thought too markedly a dilet-
tante man of letters, rather than a scholar
either in philosophy or history.

Plutarch and North must have been very
different men, yet they have a good deal in

common. Both were country gentlemen, with
a strong instinct for law and order and the
temperate morality that fits their type. They
had a strong local patriotism as well as a
wider national one and both wrote for the
edification of their own kind. But Plutarch
did not live in an heroic society; North, the
fellow of Raleigh and Humphrey Gilbert, of
Drake and Grenville, of Philip Sidney and
Francis Vere, certainly did; and Plutarch
hardly rises to the height of his own great
argument so surely as North (and Amyot)
does.

If the Langhornes or Clough translated
Plutarch more faithfully than North, it is a
measure not only of their superior knowledge of the original (and of their better
text) but of the inferiority of their age. An
Elizabethan could not translate faithfully in
the sense in which the nineteenth century
understood it. The individuality of the men
and of their language was too strong to sub-
due itself wholly to the stuff they wrought
in. North and Philemon Holland and Angel
Day and the translators of the Bible, and
even such imperfect craftsmen as Nichols,
the Tudor translator of Thucydides, are too
full-flavoured to represent truthfully the

taste of their originals. Plutarch possessed
indeed the great merit of simplicity, and
herein North resembles him, but the translator was surely a tougher, more active, deeper and more impassioned person than the
pleasant, inquisitive, garrulous historiogra-
pher. North has the air of being a more practical person than Plutarch and gifted also
with a more vivid imagination. In part it
arises from the qualities of their respective
languages, in part from their own characters,
that North tends to use more concrete language, and to keep the pictured scene more
constantly before his readers. Thus in
North's version, when the stranger suborn-
ed by Thales has told Solon that he has seen
at Athens 'a young man carried to burial,
whom all the city followed ', Solon, growing
anxious, enquires ' if he were not the son of
Solon which was buried ', recalling to our
minds the scene of the funeral procession.
Plutarch and his more literal translators
write only 'which was dead.' When the
heroic Mucius Scaevola holds his right hand
over the fire, North says that ' the flesh of
the hand did fry off.' The specifically culin-
ary word ' fry ', which gives grim point to the

phrase, is his own. Plutarch used only a general word 'burning' *(καιομένης τῆς σαρκός).*

Similarly North translates in the best sense of the term by taking over not mere words but ideas and by evoking images of like quality; Cimon's 'trireme', for example, becomes 'the admiral's galley'. He tells his anecdotes, too, with a certain freedom which makes always for simplicity and clearness; the story of the origin of the Minotaur (in the life of Theseus) is a notable example of his clear and orderly method of narration. North thus does a little, much he cannot do, to correct Plutarch's weakness for losing sight of his objective amid a fine, profuse medley of information.

Occasionally, too, North interpolates a comment which shows his acquaintance with the realities of human nature. Thus when Brutus without change of countenance suffers his own sons to be executed before his very eyes, Plutarch says that this was due either to his remarkable virtue or to his overpowering misery, which obscured all other feelings. North adds the remark that this was 'passing the common nature of man, that hath in it both divineness, and sometimes beastly brutishness '. A sentiment in which Hamlet would have concurred.

But whatever the writer of the *Lives* may have been, his theme is an heroic one and, though not a poet, he had a sufficient sincerity of emotion to pass on something of the greatness which he could not help discerning in the men whose lives he had studied. He may not have really understood them ; but at least he tells their story without overloading or obscuring it with rhetoric or false sentiment ; and just the added colour of North's style makes the portraits glow with life, while the yet rarer genius of Shakespeare, working on North's prose, makes them stir and breathe and speak.

§ 7.

Many of the qualities of North's style have been illustrated in the passages already cited. He writes clearly and forcibly; he is free in his maturer work from all tendency to preciosity, while preserving a strong feeling for rhythm and the decorative qualities of prose. He uses vernacular words and idioms with very great skill, giving point and freshness to his descriptions and to his dialogue, and constantly keeping in touch

with real life. He can be easy without being
slipshod, dignified without being pompous.
Here is a typical and straight-forward passage from *The Diall of Princes:*

> I have read in the time of King Alexander the
> great, there was a renowned Pyrate on the Sea, called
> Dyonides, the which robbed and spoiled al the
> shipping that hee could get: and by commaunde-
> ment of this good King Alexander, there was an
> armie sent foorth to take him. And when he was
> taken and presented to King Alexander, the King
> saide unto him, Show me, Dyonides, why dost thou
> so spoyle on the sea, that no ship can sayle on the
> sea out of the east into the west for thee? The pyrate
> aunswered and sayde: 'if I spoyle the sea, why
> dost thou, Alexander, rob both the sea and land
> also? O Alexander, because I fight with one shippe
> in the sea, I am called a thiefe : and because thou
> robbest with two hundreth ships on the sea, and
> troublest all the world with 200,000 men, thou art
> called an Emperour. I sweare unto thee, Alexander,
> if Fortune were as favourable to me, and the Gods
> as extreme against thee : they would give mee thine
> Empyre, and thee my little shippe: and then perad-
> venture I should bee a better king than thou art,
> and thou become a worse thiefe then I am.'
>
> These were high words, and well receyved of
> Alexander : and of truth to see if his wordes were
> correspondent to his promises, he made him of a
> pyrate a great captaine of an armie. . . .

That is very correctly and precisely worded, but easy and graceful. Very few contemporary writers could have kept even this
straightforward piece of narration so evenly
modulated and free from involution.

North uses very long sentences at times but he never allows his sense to become obscure or his construction at all tangled. He does not yield purple passages which may be effectively quoted as specimens of his ' style '. He wrote long books and his prose is of a kind that can be read without surfeit in bulk. He varies his tone to suit his subject, keeps his main argument roundly and flowingly phrased, tells his anecdotes with a proper liveliness, never lets his rhythm become mechanical or obtrusive, and uses an excellently wide and varied vocabulary. Consider such chance-picked sentences as these:

> If any good quality were lacking in him, he did so finely counterfeit it, that men imagined it was more in him than in those that naturally had it in them in deed. (Solon).

> Howbeit he advised her to go her full time, and be brought a-bed in good order, and then he would find means enough to make away with the child that should be born. (Lycurgus.)

How simple is North's language, but how exact and comely!

> But Brutus, that was a fast and resolute man, and very fierce in his heart, ran immediately into the market-place, crying out that his fellow consul was a traitor, and contented to grant the tyrants matter and means to make war upon the city, where indeed they deserved not so much as to be relieved in their exile.

It is by such inconspicuous but uniformly sound and skilful writing that North best served the cause of English prose in an age which was already tending both in poetry and in prose to over-emphasis, hyperbole, and ' conceits '.

North's is a prose that has withstood the test of time. Here are three renderings, the product of three centuries, of the same brief passage:

The Translation called DRYDEN'S revised by A. H. GLOUGH.

His temperance, as to the pleasures of the body, was apparent in him from his very childhood, as he was with much difficulty incited to them, and always used them with great moderation : though in other things he was extremely eager and vehement, and in his love of glory, and the pursuit of it, he showed a solidity of high spirit and magnanimity far above his age. For he neither sought nor valued it upon every occasion, as his father Philip did (who affected to show his eloquence almost to a degree of pedantry, and took care to have the victories of his racing chariots at the Olympic games engraven on his coin), but when he was asked by some about him, whether he would run a race in the Olympic games, as he was very swift-footed, he answered, he would, if he might have kings to run with him.

THE LANGHORNES.

His continence showed itself at an early period for though he was vigorous or rather violent in his other pursuits, he was not easily moved by the pleasures of the body ; and if he tasted them, it was with great moderation. But there was something superlatively great and sublime in his ambition, far above his years. It was not all sorts of honour that he courted, nor did he seek it in every track, like his father, Philip, who was as proud of his eloquence as any sophist could be, and who had the vanity to record his victories in the Olympic chariot-race in the impression of his coins. Alexander, on the other hand, when asked by some of the people about him, whether he would not run in the Olympic race (for he was swift of foot), answered, "Yes, if I had kings for my antagonists."

NORTH.

Even from his childhood they saw that he was given to be chaste. For though otherwise he was very hot and hasty, yet he was hardly moved with lust or pleasure of the body and would moderately use it. The ambition and desire he had of honour shewed a certain greatness of mind and noble courage, passing his years. For he was not (as his Father Philip) desirous of all kind of glory: who, like a rhetorician, had a delight to utter his eloquence, and stamped in his coins the victory at the Olympian games, by the swift running of his horses and coaches. For when he was asked one day (because he was swift of foot) whether he would assay to run for victory at the Olympian games, "I would be content" (said he) "so I might run with Kings".

There is a flabbiness about the Langhornes' prose contrasting strongly with the vigorous purposefulness of North's. 'At an early period', 'superlatively great and sublime'—the Langhornes have no certain knowledge

what 'period', and 'superlatively sublime',
mean; but they more or less contain the
required sense and they fill out the sentence
to a respectable shapeliness. North's is a
much more individual use of words. How
much more concrete and therefore vivid is
'stamped in his coins the victory at the
games' than 'record his victories in the impression of his coins.' North, too, with his
'by the swift running of his horses and
coaches' emphasizes, as the Langhornes' 'In
the Olympic chariot-race' does not, the contrast between Philip's vicariously earned
prizes and Alexander's personal prowess. The
Langhornes' 'Yes, if I had kings for my antagonists' is well enough, but how much better
is the more simply worded but more memorable phrase 'I could be content so I might run
with Kings.'

In his rendering of dialogue North is especially good. A little later in this same life
comes the account of the breaking-in of Bu-
cephalus, which Alexander is bold enough to
undertake.

'But if thou canst not, no more than they,' replied
Philip, 'what wilt thou forfeit for thy folly?' 'I
am content,' quoth Alexander, 'to jeopard the price
of the horse.'

Thus North, with a distinction of language which is yet utterly simple and almost vernacular. The Langhornes render it:

> 'If you should not be able to ride him what forfeiture will you submit to for your rashness'. 'I will pay the price of the horse.'

Correct enough but lamentably flat. The Clough-Dryden version is worse, making Alexander undertake to pay 'the whole price of the horse', as though he had meditated risking a part only, but calculated that the longer odds were justified. The Greek ἀποτίσω τὸυ ἵππου τήν τιμήν does indeed contain in the compound verb the sense of payment in full, but North's 'jeopard' holds as much and more, though perhaps not precisely what is in the Greek.

For a last comparison, set a sentence of North beside one from the latest translation of Plutarch (in the *Loeb Library*). I do not think anyone will need to be told which is which:

However, he did not suffer his democracy to become disordered or confused from an indiscriminate multitude.

Yet, for all that, he suffered not the great multitude that came thither, tag and rag, to be without distinction of degrees and orders.

As a translator there may be a little to say against North: as an artist in prose there is everything to be said for him. He wrote of heroes in an heroic style, and in an age which has itself achieved much heroism he should find understanding readers.

JOHN LYLY.

§ 1.

JOHN LYLY has suffered a strange trick at the hands of fortune. He was, I have little doubt, a light-hearted, quick-witted, somewhat mercurial person, brilliant but easily turned from his purpose, with a ready perception of the tastes of his public, but no very strong artistic ideals of his own, lighting by chance on beautiful thoughts and gifted with a most delicate ear for harmonies of word or phrase, but with no philosophy of life and no particular interest in his own technique. A featherweight, thistledown kind of man, whose beautiful creations one should enjoy without seeking to explain their mechanism and without taking their author too seriously. Most of the Elizabethan men of letters had in them somewhere a robustness, a physical solidity, which never suggests itself in Lyly's case. One can hardly imagine him settling down as a family physician or playing the retired, newly-made gentleman.

It would be as the support of such men as
Lyly that the patron (an institution in any
case over-abused) might well be justified. Unfortunately Lyly's two best patrons were
Burleigh, who was no pillar of the stage, and
Oxford, who early in his client's career lost
favour at court. Thus we find this pleasant
airy being passing his days in patnetic
appeals for material comfort to Burleigh and
the Queen till he finally disappears from
public view.

Again, Lyly, in the ripeness of his talent,
turned from the novel (if *Euphues* can be
called one) to the writing of plays, which,
though they achieved a narrower fame,
touched highwater-mark in their own special
kind, and possess a far better title to a permanent place in our literature. Yet *Euphues,*
the interest in which is related mainly to
literary history, is well known to any reader
of our older literature, and any one who has
ever sat for examination in that subject
shudders at the name, while the plays are too
often dismissed, unread, as an intluence on
Shakespeare's early and less commended
plays, and Euphuism, an exaggerated fashion
of writing which Lyly as he matured grew

steadily out of, is regarded as the essential quality of his art.

To apply the methods of pedantry to the work of such a man seems almost desecration, yet the pedants have mauled scarcely any poet more in proportion to the appreciative or sympathetic criticism he has received. Even the graceful and discriminating work of the admirable French critic M. Feuillerat is embodied in a monograph weighing no less than three and three quarter pounds!

§ 2.

The date of Lyly's birth is not exactly known, but in the matriculation list of Magdalen College, Oxford, dated October 8, 1571, he is described as being 17 years of age. I do not know that this depends on any thing better than Lyly's own assertion, but there is no reason for doubting it, so that his birth may be placed somewhere within the twelve months ending October 8, 1554.

The place of his birth and breeding and even of his parentage were for a long time equally unknown, but the researches of M. Feuillerat at length established these in a very interesting manner. His grandfather was no less a person than William Lyly (or

Lilly) the grammarian, his father one Peter
Lyly, a prebendary and later registrar of
Canterbury. His mother was a Burgh, of a
well-connected Yorkshire family.

Where he was at school, or whether he
went to school at all, is again unknown. The
first definitive statement regarding him in
the older biographies is that of Anthony
Wood, who says that

> " John Lylie, or Lylly, a Kentish man born, became
> a student in Magd. coll, in the beginning of 1569,
> aged 16, or thereabouts, and was afterwards, as I
> conceive, either one of the demies or clerks of that
> house; but always averse to the crabbed studies of
> logic and philosophy. For so it was that his genie
> being naturally bent to the pleasant paths of poetry
> (as if Apollo had given him a wreath of his own
> bays, without snatching or struggling), did in manner
> neglect academical studies, yet not so much but
> that he took the degrees in arts, that of master being
> compleated 1575. "

The University Register shows that Lyly
matriculated in 1571, took his Bachelor's
degree in 1573, and his Master's in 1575. In
1579 he was incorporated M. A. in the University of Cambridge, but there is no reason for
supposing he ever resided there.

In 1574 Lyly, in spite of his neglected studies, thought he had a claim to be a fellow of
Magdalen. The fellows would have none of
him, so Lyly appealed to Burleigh, whom he

calls his *'patronus colendissimus'*, to obtain a royal mandate for his admission to their society. The Latin in which this charming piece of impertinence is written is none of the best, and Lyly can adduce no stronger reason why Burleigh should thus foist him on his unwilling college than that he badly needs the place and has no other hope of getting it. Burleigh did not accede to his request.

We next hear of him lodging in the Savoy, by the favour of William Absolon, a fellow Cantuarian, cultivating, perhaps with some success, the patronage of his powerful neighbour, Lord Burleigh. Meanwhile he sought to make his reputation with a book, and in 1578 there appeared *The Anatomy of Wit,* the first part of what is commonly known as *Euphues.* It achieved immediate popularity, four editions being printed within fifteen months, and Lyly was prompt to press his success with a sequel, *Euphues and his England,* published in 1580. Its vogue was even greater than its predecessor's. Fifty years later Blount, the editor of Lyly's collected comedies, wrote:

"Our nation are in his debt for a new English which he taught them. Euphues and his England began first that language : All our ladies were then his Scholars, and that Beautie in Court which could

not Parley Euphueisme, was as little regarded, as
shee which now there speakes not French."

To Blount writing so long after the event
this may have appeared so. In reality
Euphuism, like French, was not a new language, though it might be one only newly
learnt by the Ladies of the Court. Nor was
the matter of *Euphues* any more novel. In all
respects *Euphues,* meaning thereby the two
books just mentioned, represents the culmin-
ation of a literary mode. It rode to success
on the top of a flood tide. Lyly's ideals of culture and education would not have startled
his own grandfather, and the book is akin to
many others of Tudor times—to the two versions of Guevara, Berners' *Golden Booke* and
North's *Diall of Princes,* to Ascham's *Schole-
master,* Elyot's *Governour,* Hoby's *Courtier*
(after Castiglione) and others; not at all
points resembling any of them, but giving a
hint now of one, now of another, and string-
ing the whole on a thread of romance, thus
catering for all classes of readers, providing
serious and edifying thoughts for Burleigh,
wit and elegant discourse for his son-in-law
Oxford, sentiment and sugared speech for the
ladies. The book is to us of immense value,
and yet of less, intrinsically, than the text

books would lead us to suppose. If *Euphues* were totally lost, literature would not have suffered over-much, and we could learn elsewhere all that it has to tell us of the spirit of the age and of the art of prose-writing in the middle of Elizabeth's reign, but we could not learn it so compendiously or so pleasantly.

§ 3.

Lyly seems to have been under no delusions as to the permanence of this kind of art. After *Euphues and his England* he never, so far as we know, attempted another book of the same sort, nor any sort of romance. The tide, he must have realized, was on the turn even while the rapidly issued editions of his second book were still being put upon the market. He did not trust to maintaining himself by such labours, but turned to another form of literature, and at the same time looked for support apart from the earnings of his pen. This may not have been really due to his wisdom, but rather to the fickleness of his fancy; two books of a kind may have exhausted his energies in that direction. If so he succeeded better than he deserved, for he cer-

tainly found the form which best suited his
genius and truly earned with his comedies
the fame which has come to him, a little
dubiously, from his romance.

Euphues and his England was dedicated to
Edward de Vere, Earl of Oxford, who had
married Ann Cecil; a brilliant but frivolous
nobleman, in whom M. Feuillerat sees 'the
purest type of the Italianate Englishman of
the age, the true *'Speculum Tuscanismi'*.
Lyly was now serving him in some capacity,
perhaps as secretary, perhaps merely as one
of his ' gentlemen ', and he was not only hereditary Grand Chamberlain and so ultimately
responsible for dramatic performances at
court, but also a play-writer and maintainer
of a company of players. Here then was a
natural avenue for Lyly to approach fame
and fortune. He turned playwright and
sought also permanent employment of some
sort in this connection.

His comedies fared well enough, though in
the nature of things they could not earn the
wide renown of his romances, even in print.
But the second of them had hardly been performed when Oxford, by a quarrel with the
Howards and their partisans, incurred the
Queen's displeasure, and Lyly himself, by ap-

pearing to sympathize with Lady Oxford in a particularly bitter quarrel between her and her husband, came under a further domestic cloud. In 1583 he married Beatrice Browne, a bride of very good Yorkshire stock.

In 1584 he resumed operations in the drama with *Gallathea,* but for some reason, probably the dissolution or the suppression of those 'little eyasses' the Children of Paul's, who were his accustomed actors, the piece was not at this time produced but published unacted. His plays were not of a type which the adult companies were well fitted to produce and they never seem to have attempted them. In this year, however, Oxford generously bestowed on him an endowment worth, in our money, some £200. a year (£30-13-4), which he compounded three years later for £250. in cash; an improvident proceeding, doubtless, but not so bad a bargain as might have been feared.

The following year saw the Paul's boys reconstituted, and three more comedies were written and acted, and *Gallathea* acted as well, before the final suppression of Lyly's young players in 1591. With this event his career as a writer of comedies comes to an end. The company was indeed revived in

1599, and the Children of the Chapel also acted at least one of Lyly's pieces; but his only
return to the stage was with a piece in which
he experimented with the now fashionable
blank verse, *The Woman in the Moone,* published, after production at court nobody
knows when, in 1595. But even before the end
Lyly was growing weary of his new craft; for
his penultimate play, *Mother Bombie,* was a
piece of a decidedly different type from its
predecessors. One other play, written in
rhymed verse and sometimes ascribed to
Lyly, *The Maid's Metamorphosis,* belongs to
the turn of the century, but it is almost certainly not his.

Lyly's writings were not such as were
likely to earn him much money, nor for the
matter of that were those of any play-wright
of the age; and the cessation of his dramatic
productions may not have affected his income
very much. But that seems never to have been
sufficient for his needs, which were not, we
may assume, of the most modest kind. He continued to the end of his life to be a courtier
and for several sessions, from 1588 to 1601,
sat in Parliament. He was continually appeal-
ing to the Cecils or to the Queen for some
kind of post in the Revels office, but there is

no precise evidence that he ever obtained anything at all, certainly not that Mastership of which he had as he thought been promised the reversion. He is indeed described in a genealogical table printed by M. Feuillerat as 'Esq. to the body to Q. Elizabeth', but there would be little solid satisfaction in the enjoyment of that honour. In his second petition to the Queen there is a punning and rather obscure allusion to 'Tents and Toyles', which Mr. Bond has interpreted to mean that Lyly had been employed as Clerk-controller of the Tents and Toils—a branch of the Revels Office, but in the face of his subsequent lament, 'Thirteen years your Highness servant : but yet nothinge... A thousand hopes, but all nothinge, a hundred promises, but yet nothinge', it is difficult to accept this. So he went on hoping (he had always ten times more hopes than even promises), till the time came for him to receive vij yards of black cloth and his servants iiij yards, to make mourning suits for the funeral of his royal mistress. Anthony Wood knew nothing of him after the year 1597. In point of fact he did not die till 1606, and then he was only 52. But his work was done and his fame achieved by the time he was 36.

Meanwhile Lyly had tried yet one other species of literature—controversial pamphleteering.

In 1588 some Puritan, under the name of Martin Marprelate, had attacked Archbishop Whitgift, Aylmer, Bishop of London, and Cooper, Bishop of Winchester, in the most violent and scurrilous pamphlets. After vain endeavours to suppress these slanderous publications, the bishops resolved to fight their opponent with his own weapons and hired some of the most noted wits of the day, notably Lyly and Nash, as Church propagandists.

I have no intention of here discussing the Marprelate pamphlets, or Lyly's share in them. Witty though they are, they are of no artistic value, and they throw little or no light on Lyly's more literary writings or on his real opinions. Suffice it therefore to record that he was, on the evidence of his quondam friend and present enemy, Gabriel Harvey, the author of *Pappe with an hatchet, Alias, a Figge for mie God sonne, Or cracke me this nut. Or a country cuffe, that is a sound boxe of the eare, for the idiot Martin to hold his peace, seeing the patch will take no warning. Written by one that dares call a dog, a dog and made to prevent Martins god daies.* (1589). He may have written the slightly earlier *A Whippe for an Ape : or Martin displaied,* and others of the series have been attributed to him. But I grudge these *ephemeria* energies that might have been devoted to the writing of more *Court Comedies.*

§ 4.

It is the manner of his writing, not his powers of construction, still less of character- ization, that bestows greatness on Lyly's dramatic pieces.

No such beautiful prose as his is to be found in Elizabethan literature, and this I maintain without any very great admiration for those qualities which are usually under- stood by the name Euphuism. From this epi- demic disease, for such it was, Lyly indeed at one time suffered, as more or less had all Europe. Ascham, writing seven or eight years before the publication of *The Anatomy of Wit,* denounced Italianate conceits:

> "It is a world to see how Englishmen desire to hear finer speech than this language will allow, to eat finer bread than is made of wheat or wear finer cloth than is made of wool. . . . . "

Marini was the most famous Italian Euphuist, but most writers there had a touch of
the complaint. In Spain it has been traced,
half a century earlier, to Guevara. In France
it mars the poetry of the Pléiade.

The disease is little more than excessive
devotion to the artifices of style, blended with
the remains of the mediaeval love of allegory,
which here appears as a too frequent and pur-
poseless use of simile. But, had it not been
carried to excess, this tendency was by no
means to be regretted. English prose had long
been left to wind along in monstrous and un-
wieldy coils; if some of Ascham's contemporaries went too far they were merely the extreme left of a band of well-intentioned and
deserving reformers. In Lyly's hands prose
acquires some of the qualities already sought
for in good poetry, qualities which should be
common to all speech, and not to verse alone—
neatness of phraseology, antithesis and
rhythm. Besides this structural reform, he
elevates the language of dramatic prose from
slang to a refined diction and adds, in accordance with the taste of the age, ornament. It
is the ornament on which critics have usually
fixed as his characteristic, and everyone
knows of what kind it is. Similes are his fa-

vourite form; borrowed for the most part from real or fabulous natural history and used often three or four at a time. But in the plays these are not nearly so common as the novels and they grow steadily fewer as time goes on. The tropes, similes and antitheses sink (according to Mr. Child's reckoning) from two and a half to the page in *Campaspe* to little more than one to two pages in *Mydas* and *Mother Bombie*. Moreover these similes are often both apt and witty; as this one in *Euphues and his England*:

> "if the envious shall clap lead to my heels to make me sinke, yet if your lordship with your little finger do but hold me up by the chinne, I shall swim and be so far from being drowned."

Humour he has, too, a commodity not over common hitherto in English prose. But his chief characteristic, apart from his technicalities of style, is his analysis of passion. Love is his favourite *motif,* and of this and of the art of flirtation he gives us a careful study. Of women he shews intimate knowledge and we can well believe that he was ever a favourite with the court ladies. To them he makes direct appeal in several of his prefaces and epilogues, and continually, by flattery, in his plays.

The order of the plays is a matter of conjecture, but the whole period which they cover is short, and in their structure and dramatic qualities there is very little growth to be traced. The dates of publication are indeed known, but it is certain that publication did not always closely follow production; nor production, composition. The following is a list of the plays, in the order in which they were probably written, with the date of first publication:

Campaspe 1584	also in Blount's *Six Court Comedies*. 1632.	
Sapho and Phao . . . 1584	"	
Gallathea 1592	"	
Endimion 1591	"	
Mydas 1592	"	
Mother Bombie 1594	"	
The Woman in the Moone 1597		
Love's Metamorphosis 1601		

All the above have been reprinted by Fairholt, and, more recently and more correctly, by Bond. Dodsley included *Campaspe*, and Dilke *Endimion, Mydas* and *Mother Bombie*, in their *Old Plays*.

§ 5.

Campaspe was produced by the Children of the Chapel at Blackfriars and at Court sometime about New Year, 1581, and was never bettered by any of the succeeding plays. It is based on an historical anecdote, not like the rest on a myth, and has perhaps more human interest than any of them. The love story of Campaspe and Apelles the Painter, with Alexander's conflicting desires for love and for glory, is well set forth and is itself dramatic. In addition, the play has Lyly's usual grace of diction and ingenuity of thought. The dialogue is, as always, lively and clever and in this case aptly enough put into the mouths of professional quibblers, Aristotle, Diogenes and other philosophers, and of their servants, who chop logic in amusing burlesque of their masters.

The style of Lyly is here at its richest; antithesis and a kind of cumulative rhetoric are used with great effect, and the piece is full of neat though not very profound epigrammatic sentences, such as these:

> It were a shame Alexander should desire to command the world if he could not command himself.
> Fortune, thou did'st never yet deceive virtue because virtue never yet did trust fortune.
> Always in absolute beauty there is something above art.

A longer passage will illustrate that cumulative, heightening effect I have spoken of:

6

Alexander. I love, Hephaestion, I love. I love
Campaspe, a thing farre unfit for a Macedonian,
for a king, for Alexander!

.   .   .   .

Hephaestion. I cannot tell, Alexander, whether the
report be more shameful to be heard or the cause
sorrowful to be believed. What, is the son of
Philip, king of Macedon, become the subject of
Campaspe the captive of Thebes? Is that minde
whose greatness the world could not containe
drawn within the compasse of an idle alluring
eie? Is the warlike sound of drum and trump
turned to the soft noise of lyre and lute? the
neighing of barbed steeds whose lowdnes filled
the aire with terror and whose breathes dimmed
the sun with smoake, converted to delicate tunes
and amorous glances ——— You love, ah grief,
but whom? Campaspe, ah shame, a maid forsooth
unknowne.

(Campaspe, II, ii.)

Two of the best lyrics in the plays occur in
this one:

> Cupid and my Campaspe played
> At cards for kisses.

and

> What bird so sings yet so does wail?

But though these songs, which have been
reprinted in countless anthologies, have
always been ascribed to Lyly, the best modern scholars have, alas, decided that he
cannot certainly be affirmed the author of
any of the lyrics in the later texts of the
plays; of which, none the less, they remain

among the chief ornaments; and we owe a
debt of gratitude to Blount for inserting
them in the text of the *Six Court Comedies.*

Sapho and Phao, a play I take less pleasure
in, is based on a pseudo-classical myth. Phao,
the ferryman of Syracuse, has taken Venus
and Cupid over in his boat and Venus, seeking to put down the beautiful Sapho, has
been hoist with her own petard and made
amorous of Phao. The ladies and gallants of
Sapho's court have much witty repartee,
always an excellent feature in Lyly. Sapho,
in love, like Venus, with the now irresistible
Phao, would rather die than confess her love,
and Lyly exercises his ingenuity in making
her vent her passion in words, but ambigu-
ously, so that Phao shall not see it. Venus,
to rid herself of Sapho's rivalry, has occasion
to visit her ill-used husband Vulcan, maker
of Cupid's bolts. She coaxes him very prettily
and he, though he knows her for a humbug,
does her will, while he and his Cyclopes sing
a song less highly esteemed than some, yet
not lacking the touch of the true lyrist :

> My shag-haire Cyclops, come lets ply
> Our Lemnian hammers lustily ;
> By my wifes sparrowes
> I sweare these arrows

6*

Shall swinging fly
Through many a wantons eye.
These headed are with golden blisses,
These silver ones feathered with kisses.
But this of lead
Strikes a clown dead.

Gallathea was entered at Stationers' Hall in 1585 and written, topical allusions would suggest, a year earlier, and played by the Children of Paul's before the Queen's Majesty on New Year's Day, 1587/8. It is perhaps a revised version that was printed in 1592 and now alone survives. Here again Lyly used classical costume and a classical myth, but the setting of the scene is Lincolnshire, and Poseidon's monster, to whom sacrifice of the fairest maiden in the countryside must be made, is the bore, or Agar, of Jean Ingelow's *High Tide on the Coast of Lincolnshire.* To protect them from this horrid fate, two maidens are disguised as boys by their fathers, and, meeting in the woods in this disguise, fall in love with one another. With this is joined the story of Cupid's adventures among Diana's nymphs, whom he inspires with love for the supposed boys, and also the adventures of three brother vagrants who try various trades. Finally, Diana induces Poseidon to forego his right and one of the

two girls is made to change her sex that they
may marry and live happily ever after.

The play has the usual Lylyan qualities
of witty dialogue and touches of charming
fancy and happy characterization. The sort
of point which Lyly makes so neatly seems
trite to us, but was fresher then and even
now would find new life on the lips of a well-
graced actor. Thus Haebe, in default of Gallathea and Phillida, is offered as the belle of
the village to Poseidon. Loud are her lamen-
tations, till the God rejects her as not pretty
enough, when she begins to desire beauty
with death rather than to be alive but
scorned.

Here is a specimen of Lyly's dialogue,
empty, perhaps, but sparkling and rapid as
a shuttle: Cupid has been captured by the
outraged nymphs:

> *Telusa.* Come, sirra, to your task. First you must
> undo all these lovers' knots, because you tied
> them.
> *Cupid.* If they be true love knots, 't is impossible to
> unknit them; if false, I never tied them.
> *Eurota.* Make no excuse, but to it.
> *Cupid* Love-knots are tied with eyes, and cannot
> be undone with hands; made fast with thoughts,
> and cannot be unloosed with fingers. Had Diana
> no task to set Cupid but things impossible? I
> will to it.
> *Ramia.* Why how now? You tie the knots faster.

Cupid. I cannot choose, it goeth against my mind to make them loose.

Eurota. Let me see—now, 'tis impossible to be undone.

Cupid. It is the true love-knot of a woman's heart, therefore cannot be undone.

Ramia. That falls in sunder of itself.

Cupid. It was made of a man's thought, which will never hang together.

Larissa. You have undone that well.

Cupid. Aye, because it was never tied well.

Telusa. To the rest, for she will give you no rest. These two knots are finely untied.

Cupid. It was because I never tied them; the one was knit by Pluto, not Cupid; by money, not love; the other by force, not faith; by appointment, not affection.

Telusa. Why do you lay that knot aside?

Cupid. For death.

Telusa. Why?

Cupid. Because the knot was knit by faith and must only be unknit by death.

Eurota. Why laugh you?

Cupid. Because it is the fairest and the falsest; done with greatest art, and least truth; with best colours, and worst conceits.

Telusa. Who tied it?

Cupid. A man's tongue.

and so on, in the best light comedy (today it would be musical comedy) vein; largely irrelevant and superficial, but gay, pointed and brisk.

Endimion, produced at Court in 1586 and printed in 1591, is one of the best of the series, though burdened with a heavy load of political allegory. Its sub-title

is *The Man in the Moone,* and it sets forth
how Cynthia, the unattainable, is beloved of
Endimion ; but Tellus, who herself loves him,
employs the witch Dipsas to cast him into a
long sleep. Cynthia thereupon imprisons
Tellus, who tempts her gaoler, Corsites, and
induces him to try to move Endimion from
the bank of lunary where he lies sleeping.
Corsites, in this anticipating the Fat Knight,
is pinched by the Fairies whose revels he
disturbs :

> Pinch him, pinch him, black and blue,
> Saucy mortals must not view
> What the Queen of Stars is doing,
> Nor pry into our fairy wooing.

At last Eumenides, Endimion's faithful
friend, obtains the privilege of having a ' re-
medie ' for any one thing. He doubts whether
to choose to have his love for Semele satisfied,
or his friend awaked, but decides on the more
generous choice. By his instructions Cynthia
then kisses Endimion, who awakes, has his
youth restored to him, and devotes his life
to the contemplation of Cynthia's beauty.
Semele, ' the very wasp of all women ' (an
ancestress of Benedick's Beatrice) grants
her hand to the loyal Eumenides.

In all this it is impossible not to suspect an
allegory, and the commentators have fur-

nished us with a jangling bunch of the most
elaborate keys, which cannot however be
profitably considered without a minute
knowledge of the court history of the time.
Cynthia is of course the Queen; Endimion is
either Leicester or James of Scotland, and
Tellus either Lady Sheffield or Mary Queen
of Scots. M. Feuillerat points out that in
1582/3 a marriage between Elizabeth and
James was being spoken of, to which Mary,
then a prisoner, would naturally be bitterly
opposed. Dipsas used commonly to be identified with the Countess of Shrewsbury, but
M. Feuillerat would explain her as the Church
of Rome. At any rate, she is the instigator,
on Mary's behalf, of attempts to embarrass
James. From these Elizabeth at last frees
him, recognizing him as her heir and bestow-
ing on him the light of her countenance.
Eumenides, in this scheme, is the Master of
Gray; the earlier commentators favoured
Lord Sussex or Sir Philip Sidney.

The minor characters depend, of course,
on the major ones and no one presumes to
identify them all. The whole matter is probably incapable of certain settlement and it
is to be regretted that interest in this puzzle
has tended to the neglect of the real beauties

of the play, which were long ago singled out
for eulogy by Hazlitt. Lyly's beautiful
speech is here seen at its best, and I cannot
withhold some characteristic sentences, together with another specimen of Lyly's
dialogue:

> Vaine Eumenides—follow thou thine own fortunes
> which creepe on the earth and suffer me to flie to
> mine whose fall though it be desperate, yet shall it
> come by daring. (*Endimion* I. i.)
>
> Semele, whose golden locks seem most curious
> when they seeme most careless. (II. i.)
>
> The love of men to women is a thing common and
> of course : the friendship of man to man is infinite
> and immortal. (III. iv.)
>
> Do not that wrong to the settled friendship of a
> man as to compare it with the light affection of a
> woman. (V. ii.)
>
> My palace is paved with grasse and tiled with
> stars. (IV. ii.)
>
> Being old before thou rememberest thou wast
> young. (IV. iii.)

> *Tellus.* But in sooth, Endimion, without more cere-
> monies, is it not Cynthia?
>
> *Endimion.* You know, Tellus, that of the Gods we
> are forbidden to dispute because theyre deities
> come not within compasse of our reasons; and
> of Cynthia we are allowed not to talke but to
> wonder, because her vertues are not within reach
> of our capacities.
>
> *Tellus.* Why, she is but a woman.
>
> *Endimion.* No more was Venus.
>
> *Tellus.* She is but a virgin.
>
> *Endimion.* No more was Vesta.
>
> *Tellus.* She shall have an end.

Endimion. So shall the world.
Tellus. Is not her beauty subject to time?
Endimion. No more than time is to standing still.
Tellus. Wilt thou make her immortal?
Endimion. No, but incomparable.
Tellus. Take heed, Endimion, lest like the wrastler in Olimpia that striving to lift an impossible weight catcht an incurable straine, thou by fixing thy thoughts above thy reach, fall into a disease without al recure! But I see thou art now in love with Cynthia.
Endimion. No, Tellus; thou knowest that statelie Cedar whose top reacheth unto the clowdes, never boweth his head to the shrubs that grow in the valley; nor Ivie that climeth up by the Elme, can ever get hold of the beames of the sunne: Cynthia I honour in all humilitie, whom none ought, or dare adventure to love, whose affections are immortall and vertues infinite. Suffer me therefore to gaze on the moone, at whom, were it not for thy selfe, I would die with wondering.

One can imagine the Queen listening complacently to her poet's latest turn of flattery; with, perchance, some other lady of the court secretly taking to her own heart the honeyed words.

A further source of interest lies in the subplot, most loosely worked in, in which we are introduced to one of the best and earliest of Elizabethan *Milites Gloriosi,* Sir Tophas, whose relationship to Armado, and even to Sir John Falstaff, leaps to the eye. It is emphasized by the presence of the saucy page Epiton, Armado's Moth (a name which occurs elsewhere in Lyly, in *Mydas)*. Sir Tophas talks a burlesque Euphuism, which shows how little Lyly regarded his own early mannerisms.

Mydas, acted probably on 6 January, 1588/9 and printed in 1592, is another excellent play. It also conceals an allegory. Mydas, whose story in the Greek myth is too well known to need repeating, is Philip of Spain. His ambition is to conquer Lesbos (England), but he fails. The power of turning all he touches to gold symbolizes the influx of wealth from the Indies, which proves a curse rather than a blessing. One critic has gone so far as to say that Pan and Apollo, between whom poor Mydas stood arbiter, are the Roman and the Reformed Churches, but this is unconvincing. Martius, the blood-thirsty general, may be Alva, but the detailed application of the allegory, as in *Endimion,* is difficult and here an even less profitable task.

Particularly puzzling, from a different point of view, is the singing contest between Pan and Apollo. At the risk of sharing the King's fate and acquiring ass's ears I must confess to a preference for Pan's song, and the fact that Mydas recants his decision and afterwards extols Apollo shows nothing of

Lyly's real opinion on the matter, but only that he did not conceive of Mydas as prepared to suffer for his artistic convictions. That Pan's song is better than Apollo's would matter little, for the authenticity of the lyrics is now denied, if we could be sure that Lyly meant Apollo's to appear the better. But not only have we here the songs in dispute, but the exact reasons for Mydas' judgment and they are to the modern critic thoroughly sound. It is thus that Pan voices his theory of poetry:

> *Pan.* Apollo, I told thee before that Pan was a God. I tell thee now againe, as great a god as Apollo. I had almost said a greater : and because thou shalt know I care not to tell my thought I say a greater. Pan feels the passions of love deeply engraven in his heart, with as faire nymphs, with as great fortune as Apollo, as Neptune, as Jove and better than Pan can none describe love. . . . . Be thou sunne still, Apollo, the shadow is fast at thy heeles. . . . . I as neare to thy love as thou to mine. A carter with his whistle and his whip in true eare, moves as much as Phoebus with his fierie chariot and winged horses. . . . .
> Believe, me, Apollo, our groves are pleasanter than your heavens, our milkmaides than your goddesses, our rude ditties to a pipe than your sonnets to a lute. Here is flat faith, amo, amas, where you cry, O utinam amarent vel non amarem. . . . .
> *Mydas.* Meethinks there's more sweetnesse in the pipe of Pan than Apollo's lute ; I brooke not

that nice tinkling of strings, that contents mee
that makes one start. What a shrillnesse came
into mine eares out of that pipe and what a
goodly noise it made! Apollo, I must neede judge
that Pan deserveth most praise.

Pan. Blessed be Mydas, worthy to be a god; these
girls whose eares doe but itch with daintinesse,
give the verdict without weighing the vertue:
they have beene brought up in chambers with
soft musick, not where I make the woods ring
with my pipe, Mydas.

This is a most admirable protest against
the artificial style of poetry ; and though it
involves Mydas in ridicule and disaster, it is
impossible to believe that it is not a sincere
personal utterance on the part of the author.
Did Lyly, I wonder, really in his heart prefer
the natural style, but being essentially a
court poet, not dare say as much outright, so
that he hedged and passed off his own criticism as the produce of Mydas' crass brain, to
see, perhaps, how it would be received?
These are the two lyrics in question. They
first appear in Blount's *Six Court Comedies:*

APOLLO'S SONG.

My Daphne's hair is twisted gold,
Bright stars a-piece her eyes do hold,
My Daphne's brow enthrones the graces,
My Daphne's beauty stains all faces,
On Daphne's cheek grow rose and cherry,
On Daphne's lip a sweeter berry,
Daphne's snowy hand but touched does melt,
And then no heavenlier warmth is felt,

My Daphne's voice tunes all the spheres,
My Daphne's music charms all ears.
Fond I am thus to sing her praise ;
These glories now are turned to bays.

PAN'S SONG.

Pan's Syrinx was a god indeed,
Though now she's turned into a reed
From that dear reed Pan's pipe does come,
A pipe that strikes Apollo dumb ;
Nor flute nor lute nor gittern can
So chant it as the pipe of Pan ;
Cross-gartered swains, and dairy girls,
With faces smug, and round as pearls,
When Pan's shrill pipe begins to play,
With dancing wear out night and day ;
The bag-pipe's drone his hum lays by,
When Pan sounds up his minstrelsy,
His minstrelsy! O base! This quill
Which at my mouth with wind I fill,
Puts me in mind though her I miss,
That still my Syrinx lips I kiss.

Lyly's plays are continually giving us the germs of lyrics. Few of the themes of the Elizabethan song books are not to be found propounded in Lyly's prose. Here is one in *Mydas :*

You be all young and fair, endeavour all to be wise and virtuous that when like roses you shall fall from the stalk you may be gathered and put to the still. (*Mydas*, II. ii.)

The next play is *Mother Bombie,* acted in 1590 and printed in 1594. It is of a different kind from any of the others, a comedy of intrigue of the classical type. Four fathers, one of them of the ' long-lost ' variety, and a foster nurse po'ssess between them three sons and three daughters. Their parents desire to pair them off one way, their own wish is to pair off another way. By the aid of four boys (the counterparts of the Terentian slaves) the fathers are deluded and ultimately appeased. The plot is cunningly devised and neatly rounded off, but the characters are unreal and there is none of the poetry and wit of the other plays. The play was probably an experiment, and Lyly did not think well enough of it to persevere on these lines. The wittiest touch is when Halfpenny, one of the ' boys ', on the discovery of his very clever plot to bamboozle his master is charged with it. 'And you, you oatmeal groat, you were acquainted with this plot?' To which the oatmeal groat modestly replies, 'Accessory, as it were'.

The Woman in the Moone is another experiment, this time in verse. On the strength of the prologue, which describes the play as ' a Poet's dream, the first he had in Phoebus' holy bower ', it has been said to be his first play; but even if we suppose it to have been written only a short time before its entry at Stationers' Hall in 1595, it might yet be so

described as being the first written in verse
and so under the traditional care of Phoebus.
The verse is neat and smooth, mainly of the
end-stopped type, but there is a good deal of
variety in the rhythm, so much, indeed, as to
be very remarkable in a play of the '70s,
which this one would have to be if it really
were earlier than *Campaspe*. For the rest
the play is a poor one,* lacking the usual
play of wit and having no court scenes and
no women except Pandora, who is by turns
under the influence of one of the seven
planets and therefore for six-sevenths of
the play very unloveable. A few lines will
serve to shew what manner of blank verse
Lyly wrote:

> Now rule Pandora, in fayre Cynthia's steade
> And ranke the moone inconstant like thyself.
> Raigne thou at women's nuptials and their birth,
> Let them be mutable in all their loves,
> Fantasticall, childish, and folish in their desires.
> *(W. in the M.,* V. i.)

Last of all, we come to *Loves Metamorphosis*, 'A wittie and courtly pastorall,
written by Mr. John Lyllie. First played by
the children of Paules, and now by the child-

---

* J. A. Symonds would like to doubt the authenticity of this play, but it was published during Lyly's
lifetime under his name. Blount did not reprint it,
but it is not a 'Court Comedy'.

ren of the Chappell. London: Printed by William Wood, dwelling by the West end of Paules, at the signe of Time, 1601 '.

The date of its composition has greatly puzzled the literary historians. It is known to have been acted in 1600 by the Children of the Chapel, but when the Children of Paules acted it is not known. Their operations were suspended from before October, 1591, to 1600, so that it would seem probable that it was written and acted before 1591. Mr. Bond thinks it was altered before being revived by the Children of the Chapel, but there is nothing to indicate this with certainty. It is nearly akin to *Gallathea,* to the action of which there are apparent allusions, but it seems to lack something of the vivacity and wit of the earlier plays .Ceres' nymphs scorn their forester lovers so utterly that they will scarcely condescend even to exchange repartee with them. Instead of repulsing them with their tongues, they take to their heels; with much credit, perhaps, to their virtue, but to the play's infinite loss.

M. Feuillerat, arguing from a reference by Ben Jonson in the Introduction to *Cynthia's Revels,* acted in 1600, to 'the *umbrae* or ghosts of some three or four plays departed

7

a dozen years since . . . . seen walking on your
stage here ', puts the first performance of the
play back to 1588 or thereabouts. This seems
a probable suggestion, and the plain inferiority of the play might well account for Lyly's
neglect to publish it earlier and also for his
abandonment of the theatre, wherein, too,
other names were now coming to eclipse his.

§ 6.

Chief among them, of course, is the great
name of Shakespeare. The instances of resemblance between passages in Shakespeare
and in Lyly are so many as to make a debt
owing by one to the other indisputable, and
besides these special borrowings there are
certain qualities and types of character
which originate with Lyly. Shakespeare's
early plays abound in Euphuism, which,
whether or no it derived any peculiar qualities from Lyly's wit, was certainly first introduced by him to the stage. Ladies-in-wait-
ing, courtiers, pert pages and nymphs are
Lyly's usual speakers, and he delights in
situations where *double entente* may be employed, such as that provided by the two
girls disguised as boys in *Gallathea*. *Love's*

*Labour's Lost, Much Ado about Nothing, As
You Like It* and *Twelfth Night* remind us in
many ways of Lyly; and though in their
humanity and even in their construction they
are on a different plane from Lyly's, in sheer
verbal wit and that unreal brilliance which is
associated, to use a more modern instance,
with characters of the Cherubino type, characters portrayable piquantly and effectively
by boy actors, in these Shakespeare never
surpassed his predecessor. And in this respect
Lyly is unique : nowhere else did Shakespeare fail to outstrip his teachers.

There is no genuine dramatic force in
Lyly's plays, for of action there is little or
none and the characters only in flashes display individuality. But the wit, the verbal
felicity, the analysis of emotion and the satirical comment on humanity, though set forth
rather by precept than example, are inimitable and the whole conception of the plays is
beautifully uniform—setting, characters and
dialogue, a plot blended of allegory and love-
intrigue, a diction blended of metaphor and
lyric warmth.

Of his prose style abundant examples have
been quoted. His is a figured, coloured style,
but not, at its best, garish or over-elaborat-

ed. Even in *Campaspe,* the earliest of the
series, there is no empty, mechanical quality
about it, such as the parodists of Euphuism
affect. It is a modulated, carefully phrased
speech; aiming at beauty, where beauty is its
theme, at pointedness and emphasis harmo-
nizing with the speaker's character. Lyly
was no Grub Street hack, writing of a courtly
world which he know only as a gaper from
afar. He was a gentleman of the bed-chamber,
the darling of the court ladies. His pert
pages, his arch maidens, his finely-spoken
gentlemen, all are copied from the life,
though only so far as their words and outward manners go. Of their true characters
and motives we get few glimpses. But Lyly's
dialogue is, we may feel sure, the sublimation
of court parleying—neater, brighter, more
delicate than the real thing.

Concerning the mechanical properties and
rhetorical devices of his style more than
enough has been printed : the reader who
cares for such dissection may pleasurably do
it for himself. Instead, I present one more
passage, from a part of Lyly's dramatic work
not as yet touched on, those prologues and
epilogues, mellifluous but necessarily formal
and a little stilted, of which every play has

one or more. Here is the Epilogue to *En-dimion* :

> A man walking abroad, the wind and sun strove
> for sovereignty, the one with his blast, the other
> with his beames. The wind blew hard, the man
> wrapped his garment about him harder. It blustered
> more strongly, he then girt it fast to him : I cannot
> prevail said the wind. The sun casting her crystal
> beams, began to warm the man : he unloosed his
> gowne : yet it shined brighter : he then put it off.
> I yield, said the wind, for if thou continue shining,
> he will also put off his coat.

> Dread Sovereign, the malicious that seek to overthrow
> us with threats, do but stiffen our thoughts, and make
> them sturdier in storms : but if your Highness vouchsafe
> with your favourable beams to glance upon us, we
> shall not only stoop, but with all humility lay both
> our hands and hearts, at your Majesties' feet.

In his own sphere Lyly is master : no other
poet has given us anything of quite the same
charm. All the other forms of early drama,
the tragedy of blood, the chronicle play, the
low farce, were improved upon in their own
kind by Shakespeare and the later dramatists.
Lyly's court comedy springs into existence
ready armed with quip and crack, shepherd's
crook and powderpuff. To *Campaspe, En-dimion* and *Mydas* must belong the praise
of being the best of their kind, and that a
singularly beautiful one.

LANCELOT ANDREWES.

§ 1.

IN THAT same Cathedral Church of St. Saviour's, Southwark, where lies the poet Gower is the tomb of Lancelot Andrewes. It stands in the south ambulatory, and has been newly restored and coloured. Of very pleasing appearance was Andrewes, if this image is to be believed, his features cleanly made but not very large, trim moustache, small beard—a handsome man, refined and well-kept. Beside the tomb is hung a notice beginning thus:

READER.*

If thou art a Christian stay, it will be worth thy tarrying to know how great a man lies here; an incomparable bulwark of the Church of Christ, by his conversation, writings, prayers and examples.

There is no danger of the name of Lancelot Andrewes being forgotten. His *Preces Priva-*

---

* This is a translation of the Latin epitaph by Bishop Wren.

tae have taken rank as one of the devotional classics of Christianity, and he is regarded as a notable specimen of the learned, moderate Anglican divine of the pre-Laudian age. But to his own generation the *Preces* were unknown, and of Anglican bishops they had not yet a long enough line fully to appreciate his merits. To them he was *Stella Praedicantium,* 'The Planet of Preachers', and by virtue of his *XCVI Sermons* he still deserves an honourable mention among the masters of our language.

§ 2.

Lancelot Andrewes was not of such stock as usually yields Anglican bishops. For he came from London's sailor-town, being born (in 1555, the year of the burning of the Oxford martyrs) in Thames Street, Barking, ' of honest and godly parents, who besides his breeding in learning, left him a sufficient patrimony and inheritance.' His intellectual quality was discovered by his first schoolmaster, Samuel Ward, of the Coopers' Free Grammar School, Ratcliffe, who induced Lancelot's parents to suffer him to continue at school instead of being bound 'prentice. Next, Richard Mulcaster won him to come to the Merchant Taylors' School, whence he proceeded to Pembroke Hall, Cambridge, of which he became a fellow in 1576 and Master in 1589. He attracted the favourable notice of several men of importance, notably of Walsingham. He was a mighty linguist, reputed to know 15 tongues, and a patristic theologian, the most learned and deeply read of his age and nation, and in scholarship lay his chief interest. 'His late studying by candle and early rising at four in the morning, procured him envy among his equals.'

For affairs of Church discipline or of State he had evidently little taste, and though King James used him, as he used every scholar he could lay hands on, for controversial purposes, and he acquitted himself creditably therein, he was never a strong party man. When he came to be of the Privy Council it is recorded that he would speak his mind on church matters but 'meddled little in civil and temporal affairs'.

Of Andrewes' position as a theologian and as a churchman little or nothing need here be said. He believed in the essential connection between Church and State, as the twin manifestation of God's power on earth. His theology was based on authority, and in one

of his sermons he defines the source of this
authority as being 'one canon reduced to
writing by God himself, two testaments,
three creeds, four general councils, five centuries and the series of the Fathers of that
period—the three centuries that is before
Constantine and two after—as determining
the boundaries of our faith.' In other words
he was an orthodox Anglican Catholic after
the Elizabethan pattern, equally anti-puritan
and anti-papist, and in private decidedly
partial to ritual. His chapel at Ely was
famous for its appointments and its devotional atmosphere, and Laud is said to
have copied many of his arrangements.

From 1586, when he became Chaplain to
Queen Elizabeth, Andrewes was always in
close touch with the court, and he filled
successively the offices of Canon of St.
Paul's, Canon and later Dean of Westminster, Bishop of Chichester, Bishop of Ely,
and Bishop of Winchester, as well as Dean of
the Chapel Royal, where his immediate
successor was Laud. The most part of his
income he spent in charity and on restoring
the churches and other buildings in his
charge. He died in 1626.

We have our most interesting glimpses of him at Westminster and at Ely. At Westminster he showed, what was not calculated altogether to improve his sermons, his love of teaching. Hacket, Bishop of Salisbury and biographer of Dean Williams, describes how Andrewes would take a class in Westminster School for a week, would have boys to the Deanery from 8 to 11 in the evening to teach them Greek and Hebrew, and on other occasions would take some of them for a walk with him, wherein he would combine exercise with instruction.

At Ely we get an interesting view of him through the eyes of the celebrated Isaac Casaubon, second only to Scaliger among the scholars of that day, who was in England from 1609 to his death in 1614. Casaubon, who spoke no English, found in him not only a fellow student but a most serviceable friend, and he stayed with him for a considerable time at Downham.

Another continental friend was Grotius, and in England he was naturally in close touch with the antiquarian circle of Selden and Camden. It was his lament that there was no published collection of 'Histories and Decrees of Synods' in England that instigated Sir Henry Spelman to one of his tasks. An even more notable friend was Bacon, with whom he was intimate.

§ 3.

There is only one regrettable incident in Andrewes' not very eventful life, his voting for the nullification of the marriage of the Earl and Countess of Essex, a discreditable piece of court scandal according to modern standards. In excuse for Andrewes it has been said that to have voted with the minority would have been a useless risking of the King's favour. But this is as little creditable to a bishop, whose conduct should be guided by something higher than expediency, as hearty agreement with the motion. Moreover, Andrewes was not a time-server. There is a story (preserved by the poet Waller) of his sturdy dissent from his brother of Durham in his compliance in the matter of royal levies on episcopal property, and it is recorded that his very presence was enough to keep the King's unruly member from undue licence. The probability is that Andrewes, who like most of the theologians of his age held what are now regarded as exaggerated views of the sanctity of the royal prerogative, treated the matter, as he was fairly entitled to do, as one of pure law and not of morality; and in law the soundness of the decision is at least arguable. The genuineness of Andrewes' piety and practical benevolence are established by every other page in his biography, and it is incredible that a man of such character, though being human he was liable to an error of judgment, should have deliberately taken a hand in a base action which he knew to be illegal. He certainly tried to avoid having to take part in the proceedings, but being compelled to attend he was, as the most learned canon lawyer of the day, less likely than the Archbishop and the other voters in the minority to allow his moral repugnance to the motive of the suit and the character of the parties to prejudice his judgment on the point of law.

§ 4.

Mark Pattison speaks of Andrewes as 'a prelate who if he had not been a bishop might have left an eminent name in English literature'. There seems no reason why even a bishop should not attain this distinction. Indeed, even if Lancelot Andrewes be not held to have done so, his younger contemporary, Jeremy Taylor, certainly did. Nor is it enough to say that Andrewes was always a bishop either in *esse* or in *posse,* whereas the other literary bishops or deans attained office in recognition of un-ecclesiastical labours. Nor, again, that he was a court bishop, occupied with affairs and royal ceremonies, and unable on that account to find time for literature.

The fact is Andrewes had no itch to be a man of letters. He was in a broad sense a schoolmaster, and I do not know that any great schoolmaster has ever written a great book. The spoken word and the inspiring personality have always been his vehicle of expression, the minds and characters of his pupils his 'best piece of poetry'. He taught in his early days at Cambridge, and he continued, as we have seen, to teach the young whenever he had the opportunity. He taught the King and he taught his courtiers, both by his sermons and by his conversation. He must have written out many of his sermons, but did not so far as we know publish them. They were printed, after his death, by the King's Command. His *Preces Privatae* were never intended for any one's use save his own. One or two papers on theological subjects which

he wrote he did not publish. His four controversial pieces, which were written for publication, were composed in Latin and undertak-
en at the express command of King James,
who could not afford to leave his profound
knowledge of the Fathers unemployed in the
great disputation with Cardinal Bellarmine
and other Romanists concerning the Royal
authority in church matters.

To the power of the great preacher's eloquence we have the testimony of men of very
different temperaments, not only of his fellow
divines such as Isaacson and Fuller, but of
Philistines as well. Nash, the ribald and
reckless young pamphleteer, in *Have With
You to Saffron Walden,* both praises him himself and indicates another interesting
admirer, Lyly the Euphuist, no mean judge
of choice language:

'By Doctor Andrewes own desert and
Master Lillie's immoderate commending him,
by little and little I was drawne on to bee an
auditor of his : since when, whensoever I
heard him, I thought it was but hard and scant
allowance that was given him, in comparison
of the incomparable gifts that were in him.'

Another witness not easily pleased, one
would imagine, with a sermon is Sir John

Harington, who in 1608 wrote a short account
of Andrewes, published nearly fifty years
later in a work entitled *A Brief View of the
State of England.* He praises the tendency of
Andrewes' sermons to 'raise a joint reverence to God and the prince, to the spiritual
and civil magistrate', and says, with particular reference to the second Lenten sermon,
that it 'does not go in at one ear and out at
the other'.

It is generally agreed that Andrewes'
delivery was extraordinarily fine, and it is
sometimes suggested that it was to this that
his sermons owed the greatest part of their
reputation. The written text does indeed constantly suggest to the attentive reader a
voice of great power and modulation, able to
utter parallel sentences with growing emphasis, to keep some key-word ever ringing
in the ear, to enforce contrasts and simili-
tudes by the skilful modulation of its tones.
But this does not diminish our praise of the
preacher who could thus perfectly deliver
his intellectual concepts, or of the writer
who could so skilfully reproduce on paper
his own fluid eloquence.

But printed the sermons were, in 1629,
when Andrewes had lain three years in his

grave, by order of Charles I. The editors were
Laud, then Bishop of London, and Buckeridge, Bishop of Ely, and in dedicating the
collection to the King they wrote:

'We here present to your most Sacred Majestie,
a book of Sermons. We need not tell whose they
are, the sermons are able to speak their author.
When the author died, Your Majesty thought it not
fit his sermons should die with him . . . . . And
though they could not live with all that elegancie
which they had upon his tongue, yet you were
graciously pleased to thinke a paper life better than
none . . . . . There came to our hands a world of
Sermon notes, but these came perfect. Had they not
come perfect, we should not have ventured to adde
any limme unto them . . . . .'

From this it may be inferred that Andrewes
was by no means in the habit of writing
out all his sermons, and those we have
are almost all those delivered on cere-
monious occasions before the Sovereign.
Whether therefore we really have the best
of Andrewes' sermons is open to question.
Evidently their author did not write these
out fair from any desire to commend them to
posterity, but because either he would bestow
greater pains on these sermons or because he
had to be particularly careful what he said
(for both Elizabeth and James were learned
sovereigns and critical) and be able to explain
his doctrine to his Royal patron afterwards.

8

One would rather expect to get more impassioned oratory and more sincere emotion where the preacher gave himself head; though it is improbable that Andrewes at any time contented himself with rendering no more than the written version. The popular pulpit of the age was at Paul's cross, where Master Hugh Latimer had preached 'of the plough', and Andrewes must have filled this pulpit too, and filled it to the satisfaction of his audience, else he could never have achieved his immense reputation.

Nor does a study of the *XCVI Sermons* lead me to regard Andrewes as an entirely academic preacher. Certainly he always makes use of an enormous amount of learning, quoting parallel passages and instances for every phrase and allusion in his text; but his chief source after all is the Bible, that new-found heritage of the English people, which every one could now read with a freshness of perception impossible to the reader of today, whose ears are inured to its true potency. Nothing is more conspicuous in his language than his skilful and accurate use of colloquial English. However deep or however subtle his argument, his language is invariably simple, vigorous and full-flavoured. Indeed he seems deliberately to eschew the poetic manner of Donne, whose best passages have an emotional quality and a grandeur of form which impresses us today from the printed page as deeply as it did his audience. You cannot profitably take single sentences or passages in Andrewes out of their context. Andrewes suggests comparison with an architect rather than with a monumental mason. He piles up argument on argument, instance on instance, subdividing and subsuming, with a reiterated phrase or word for ever coming in like a tolling bell and marking the central idea of the whole.

Moreover he is such a master of rhythm and of the harmonies of language as easily accounts for the admiration of Lyly. His key-words are always sonorous; you can imagine the voice of the preacher ringing them forth. You begin to expect them, and by carrying on his waves of sound a little longer he postpones the fulfilment and heightens the anticipation of your aural pleasures.

'*Love* first: what moveth the *mother* to all the travail and toil she taketh with her *child?* She *hopes* for nothing, she is in years (suppose); she shall not live to receive any benefit by it : it is Love and Love only. *Love* first.

8*

> And then *hope:* what moveth the *Merchant,* and
> so the *Husbandman,* and so the *Military-man,* and
> so all the rest? All the sharp showers and stormes
> they endure, they *love* them not : it is *hope* and hope
> only of a rich return . . . . .'

In that second Lenten sermon, preached
before Queen Elizabeth in 1690, which Harington so praised, the text gives us the key-
note—'Thou diddest lead thy people like
sheepe by the hands of Moses and Aaron.'

He proceeds to consider his text word by
word, in three parts ; first, 'Thou, God '.

> To begin with God ; who beginneth the verse, by
> whom and to whom we lead, and are led, and in
> whom leading both beginneth and endeth.

Note how ' lead ' rings through the sentence. Three things there are, he goes on,
which, distinguish God.

> The first is in duxisti—thou didest lead . . . . .
> diddest then and doest still. God hath a prerogative,
> that he is *Rex a Saeculo,* and *Rex Saeculorum,* was
> our King of old and shall be our King for ever and
> ever.
> The second is in *Populum Tuum,* thy people . . .
> God's leading hath no marches. This people and all
> people are His . . . . . .
> The third is, *Per Manus,* by the hands. For as
> He guideth the people by the hands, so he guideth
> the hands themselves, by which he guideth; ruleth
> by them, and ruleth them; ruleth by their hands,
> and ruleth in their hearts: is both the shepherd of
> Israel, leading them like a sheep, and further
> leadeth Joseph also (their leader) *Tamquam Ovem,*
> like a sheep . . . . . Why then, *Dicite in Gentibus,*

Tell it out among the Nations (saith the prophet) that God is King; that he is the Tu, the Leader, the perpetual, the universal, principal Leader of his people.

Then he starts off again considering the double use of *rule* for comfort and for fear. Then, to consider the supernatural nature of rule—an ingenious but dangerous argument this, for it depends on the admission that men are *not* by nature like sheep, and that only divine power could make them so. And so again he comes back to his refrain:

Let us see God sensibly in it, and the power of God, yea the miraculous power of God; and say with the prophet, *Thou art God that doest wonders, Thou leddest thy people like Sheepe by the hands of Moses and Aaron.* And so much for the first part, first word, and person.

He proceeds to the second consideration, the full compass of the word *Leading.* Here he raises four points: ' For that it be a leading, it must be *orderly* without straying, *skilfully* without erring, *gently* without forcing, and *certainly* without missing our journey's end.' Beginning from the second point I would quote a passage of some length as a specimen, since the text is not easily accessible, of Andrewes' style.

'Now this *right way,* if we consider where it lieth, the Prophet will tell us, *Thy way O God is in the Sanctuary;* (that is) it is the word of God which is the *Load-star,* when God is the *Leadsman. Sicut oves* it must be, and this is the voice of the true Shepherd, to be listened to of all his flock, that will not rove and run headlong into the Wolf's den. This is the *Pillar of the Cloud* in regard of this people here, to be kept in view of all those that will not perish in the wilderness, wherein is no path. Indeed it is both: the *Pillar of the cloud* before directing us in the way, and the *voice of the Shepherd behind us* (as *Esay* saith) telling us when we misse, and crying, Haec est via, ambulate in ea, This is the way, the right way, walk in it.

And in this way, our guiding must be mild and gentle : else it is not *Duxisti,* but *traxisti;* drawing and driving, and no leading. *Leni spiritu non dura manu,* rather by an inward sweet influence to be led, than by an outward extreme violence to be forced forward. So did God lead his people here. Not the greatest pace (I wis) for they were a *year* marching that they might have posted in *eleven days* (as Moses saith.) No, nor yet the nearest way neither. as Moses telleth us. For he fetched a compass divers times, as all wise governors by this example must do, that desire rather *safely* to *lead,* than *hastily* to *drive* forward. The *Spirit* of God *leadeth* this people (saith Esay) *as an horse is ridden downe the hill into the valley ;* which must not be a gallop, lest horse and rider both come downe one over another ; but *warily* and easily. And *sicut oves* still giveth us light, seeing the Text compareth it to a sheep gate. Touching which kind of cattle to very good purpose, Jacob (a skilful shepherd) answereth Esau (who would have had Jacob and his flocks have kept company with his *hunting* pace.) Nay, not so, Sir, (said Jacob) it is a *tender cattle* that is under my hands, and must be softly driven, as they may endure ; if one *should over-drive them but one day,* they would all *die,* or be laid up for many days after. Indeed, Rehoboam left ten parts of his flock behind, only for ignorance of this very point in *Duxisti.* For, when in a boisterous manner he chased them before him, telling them what *yokes* he would make for them, (a far unmeet occupation for a Prince to be a *yoke-maker*) they all shrunk from him presently, and falsified his *prophecie* clean. For whereas he told them sadly, *His little finger should be as big as his Father's whole body,* it fell out clean contrary; for his *whole body,* proved not so big as his fathers *little finger.* A *gentle leading* it must be; and in the beginning, such was the course. Therefore ye have Kings of Canaan in Genesis, for the most part called by the name of Abimelech (that is) *Pater Rex,* a *King* in place, a *Father* in affection. David himself, who full bitterly complaineth, *Ah these sonnes of Zeruiah are too hard* too full of *execution* of mee. And (to end this point) thus describeth he his good Prince (in the 72 Psalme) He shall come down (not like hailstones on a house top, but) like the dew into a fleece of wool (that is) sweetly and mildly, without any noyse or violence at all. '

Lastly, in this section, he considers the end of God's leading, to the Sanctuary on earth to His own rest in heaven.

The third part in like manner considers the words *tuum populum,* thy people. For the *populus* alone, he says, ' surely no evil can be said to much of it. But *tuus* makes amends. It is not enough that they be '*Freemen* and not *Villaines; Athenians* or *Englishmen* (that is a civill) not a barbarous people.... but that they be God's *own people* and flock.' So

he returns to *sicut oves* and shows the
people's need for a guide and ruler, and
finally passes on to by the hands of Moses and
Aaron, speaking with excellent moderation
(with Elizabeth sitting under him) of the
divine origin of monarchy, which replaced
theocracy, of the responsibility of princes to
God (under three heads), and of the distinct
duties implied in the two persons of Moses,
the civil power, and Aaron, the ecclesiastical ;
again under three heads. He concludes with
no very elaborate peroration :

> The Lord by whose Almighty power all govern-
> ments do stand ; those especially wherein the people
> are *led* in the *way of his sanctuary*, as he hath
> graciously begun to *lead* us in that way, so leave us
> not, till we have finished our course with joy. Knit
> the hearts of Moses and Aaron that they may join
> lovingly: teach their hands, and fingers of their
> hands, that they may *lead skilfully*: touch the
> *hearts* of the people, that they may be led willingly ;
> that, by means of this happy conduct, surely without
> error, and safely without danger we may lead and
> be led forward, till we come to the fruition of His
> promise, the expectation of our blessed hope, even
> the eternal joys of the celestial Kingdom, through
> Jesus Christ our Lord.

Andrewes is often criticized as being a
juggler with words, a quibbler, tracing false
analogies and making over-subtle distinctions. It is easy, even from so small a frag-
ment as the passage quoted, to see the reason

for this disparagement. Andrewes so invariably finds his three or four ways of considering any text, and works round so ingeniously
to his starting point through a perfect
Chinese puzzle of sub-divisions, that we are
naturally inclined to suspect a mechanical and
insincere method. But his distinctions are not
really quite so subtle as his somewhat elaborate and formidable schematization would
suggest, and a writer of less scholarly habit,
who articulated his material less carefully,
and left out the first, second and thirds, the
I. I.s and I. 2.s, as Andrewes quite easily
could without altering his logical process,
would have escaped a good deal of this
censure.

Mark Pattison speaks slightingly of Andrewes' ' cavil and passion for verbal victory '.
It is true that he makes great play with the
meanings of words and brings two passages
together, away from their context, on the
strength of a single word in common. But in
an age which still held fast by the literal inspiration of the Bible, this exact study of
words was an all important part of scriptural
exegesis, and a ' verbal victory ' was a very
real one. To despise the value of such labour
is to despise the motive of the best scholar-

ship of the age, from the work of Erasmus to
that of Pattison's own hero, Casaubon. The
Puritans might be content with the acceptance of a truth by their own instinct or
reason. The Catholic theologian, Roman or
Anglican, had to show that his doctrine
squared with that of the Early Fathers and
the Bible. And all argument on that fruitful
theme was idle, as the scholar knew, unless
the meaning of every individual word was
exactly ascertained. And behind that, as too
few realized, lay the important problems of
textual criticism. In this last field Andrewes
worked, so far as we know, but little ; but he,
with his unrivalled knowledge of tongues,
would have been wrapping his talent in a
napkin had he not used it in the making of his
sermons.

As an interpreter of scripture, both by
exact explanation and by imaginative recon-
struction, Andrewes is magnificent. He
drives his teaching home too by the notable
vividness and unaffectedness of his language.
He may give a very latin air to his page by
his continual quotations, but he always translates them and they often contribute immensely to the sound and rhythm of his prose. It
must be remembered too that in the absence

as yet of the Authorized version the Latin
was the only text on which a scholar could
well base his arguments (without, of course,
having recourse to the Hebrew or Greek
originals). And the audience before whom
these sermons were preached, not least Elizabeth or James, would be well acquainted
with Latin. But otherwise his language is
pure, racy English. He touches often on
matters of topical interest, and not only
shows great ingenuity in relating them to
his text, but really makes them throw light
the one upon the other. Often, too, he uses
his ready command of scripture very wittily,
a trait of which the best example is to be
found not in a sermon but in *Tortura Torti,*
his attack, executed by royal command, on
Matthaeus Tortus, alias Cardinal Bellarmine:
'The pope ignores the charge "Feed my
Sheep"; he prefers to act on the injunction,
"Arise, Peter, kill and eat"'.

§ 5.

Besides the *XCVI Sermons,* which attained
great popularity and were several times reprinted, three pieces of Andrewes' handiwork
deserve mention.

Of *Tortura Torti* (1609) or the other shorter
controversial pieces *(Responsio ad Apolo-
giam Cardinalis Bellarmini* (1610) and the
posthumous *Answers to Cardinal Perron)*
nothing more need be said. His contemporaries esteemed them as well done, but if Andrewes had written nothing but works of this
nature he would have no fame today. His
Preces Privatae are written in Latin, Greek,
and Hebrew, not at all in English, and their
interest here lies in the irrefutable evidence
they afford of the genuineness of their
author's Christianity. If to any reader the sermons ever gave an impression of their
author as anything short of the sincerest, most
modest and most pious of men, the existence
of this wholly personal book of devotions
might assure him that the impression was a
false one. Buckeridge's Funeral Sermon
supplies us with an apt commentary on this
aspect of Andrewes' character :

> His life was a life of prayer. A great part of five
> hours every day did he spend in prayer and devotion
> to God. . . And when his brother Master Nicholas
> Andrewes died, he took that as a certain sign and
> prognostication and warning of his own death, and
> from that time till the hour of his dissolution, he
> spent all his time in prayer ; and his prayer book,
> when he was private, was seldom out of his hands ;
> and in the time of his fever and last sickness,

besides the often prayers which were read to him, in which he repeated all the parts of the confession and other petitions, with an audible voice, as long as his strength endured, he did (as was well observed by certain tokens in him) continually pray to himself, though he seemed otherwise to rest or slumber: and when he could pray no longer *voce*, with his voice, yet *oculis et manibus*, by lifting up his *eyes* and *hands* he prayed still; and when *nec manus, nec vox officium faciunt*, both voice and eyes and hands failed in their office; then *corde*, with his heart, he still prayed, until it pleased God to receive his blessed soul to himself.

Lastly, it must not be forgotten that Lancelot Andrewes was one of those who, sitting in Jerusalem Chamber, prepared the Authorized version of the Pentateuch and the earlier Historical Books, and in view of his great reputation as a linguist and as a master of language, it cannot be doubted that he had a main hand in the shaping of that crowning glory of English prose. The rhythm and majesty of language which came to the ears of the revisers from their forerunners were not likely to suffer any impairment at the hands of Lancelot Andrewes. The parallelism which is so marked a feature of both the poetical portions of the English Old Testament and of Andrewes' oratory, is traceable to the original Hebrew of the former. No writer more constantly reproduces the effect

of such a passage as, ' at her knees he bowed,
he fell, he lay down: at her feet he bowed, he
fell: where he bowed, there he fell down
dead ', but on a larger scale, the reiteration
spread over a whole paragraph and not compressed into a single sentence. Dip into his
Sermons and on any page you will find prose
of this texture :

> God afflicted some in *mercie* : and others in *wrath.*
> This was in His *wrath.* In his wrath God is not
> alike to all ; some he afflicteth in His more *gentle*
> and mild ; others in His *fierce wrath.* This was in
> the very fierceness of *His wrath* . . . . .
> The Cause then in God was *wrath.* What caused
> this wrath? God is not a wroth but with sin. Nor
> grievously wroth but with *grievous sin.* And in
> Christ there was no grievous sin. Nay, no sin at
> all. God did it (the Text is plain). And in his fierce
> wrath He did it. For what cause? . . . . .

Andrewes' Sermons do not, as I have said,
show to advantage in selections, and the
modern reader is not likely to take kindly to
them *in extenso* There is then little chance
of their recovering their place as a living
classic. But Andrewes deserves that high
commendation due to the artist who makes of
a thing of utility a thing of beauty, not dimin-
ishing but rather enhancing the utility by
his pains. Therefore, whether thou art or art
not a Christian, ' stay, it will be worth thy
tarrying to know how great a man lies here.'

JOHN BARCLAY.

§ 1.

IT IS one of the ironies of literary history that so many books for which their authors hoped to secure a longer life and a wider fame by writing them in Latin have by that act been doomed to an ever darkening obscurity. It is a further irony that this obscurity should have been so complete in spite of the hours that generations of youths have devoted to the study of that very Latin tongue. For the number of books, in mediaeval and even in modern literature, written in Latin is very large and the quality is high. Without reckoning the philosophers, theologians and lawyers, who to this day do some small traffic in the Roman tongue, there is a very respectable body of poetic and dramatic and historical literature, and even of fiction, lost to the generality of its natural readers by this unhappy preference for what was once an universal language. Many even of those who achieved greatness in English or in Scots sought a double fame and in doing so lost half their labour.

For even the professed scholar seldom reads a line of modern Latinity. The very name of the author of the once famous *Colloquies* would be unknown to the grammar school boy of today did it not chance to furnish a rhyme for *chiasmus*. Not many perhaps read John Gower's *Confessio Amantis* (of which only the title is in Latin); hardly any even of those reads his *Vox Clamantis*. Thomas Campion, that lyrical musician, expended his best skill on his Latin pieces. So did Cowley, the most admired poet of his age. Even Milton wrote much verse, as well as prose, in Latin. George Buchanan, one of the greatest names in Scottish literary history, wrote in no other tongue. An immense amount of talent in the great age of English drama used the language as well as the methods of Plautus and Seneca. All wrote on sand. In Latin More wrote his *Utopia,* Camden his *Britannia,* Selden his *Mare Clausum.* Bacon apologized for writing his *Essays* in English and used Latin for his more valued pieces. In Latin did that later Barclay, Robert the Quaker,

write his famous *Apologia,* and in Latin
John Barclay, the subject of this sketch,
the most illustrious Scottish man of letters
of his generation, wrote all his admirable
verse and his two famous prose " romances ".

And to such extent did these writers, and
a host of others like them, trust to the permanent vogue of their medium that they
themselves as a rule took no step to get their
works, even in prose, translated into their
native tongue.

§ 2.

William Barclay, the father of John, was an
Aberdonian by descent and at the time of his
marriage was at some pains to prove the
nobility of his birth. William Barclay was a
staunch partisan of Mary Stuart and migrated to Paris in 1571. Thence he was invited by
Charles I., Duke of Lorraine, to Pont-à-
Mousson as Principal of the School of Civil
Law. Here, in 1582, John was born; one of
twins, of whom the other, also a boy, died
young. His mother was one Anna de Male-
ville. He studied at his father's University
of Pont-à-Mousson and at Leyden under
Justus Lipsius, and became at an early age
a proficient Latin scholar, putting forth in

9

1601 at Pont-à-Mousson, a commentary on the *Thebais* of *Statius*. He was now 19.

Two years later we find him in London ; attracted thither, it is likely, by the scholarly reputation of his countryman, the new King James I, for whom he wrote a *Carmen Gratulorum* (1603). William Barclay is said to have come with him, but this is not certain, and he did not in any case remain long. It was in London that the first part of *Euphormionis Satyricon,* a Latin Romance of a scholarly picaresque type, was published, in 1603, with a dedication to James I. In 1605 John was in Angers, where his father for about a year before his death occupied the chair of Law. Here he is said to have been at work on the second and more personal book of the *Satyricon.* In that year he was married, in Paris, to one Louise Debonnaire, the daughter of a paymaster in the French Army. By her he is said to have had two sons and a daughter. In the pleasant little sketch of her in one of his Latin poems there is mention of only two children, but a second son seems to have been born later, in Rome. Only the elder son, the Abbé Barclay, born in 1609, figures in history.

In this same year, 1605, appeared the Paris edition of the first part of the *Satyricon*, the earliest now extant. The Gunpowder Plot occasioned a short pamphlet first published in Amsterdam (1606) and reprinted in the Elzevier editions of *Euphormionsi Satyricon*.

In 1606 he was back in London, enjoying the favour of James I, and we may suppose studying statecraft in no mean school. James is said to have sent him on diplomatic missions to the Emperor Rudolph, to Matthew of Hungary and to Emmanuel Philibert of Savoy. He wrote verses in Latin to Prince Henry and to Robert Cecil, to whom also he dedicated the second part of the *Satyricon* published in 1607. Of these verses he published a collection entitled *Sylvae*, which he dedicated to yet another distinguished recipient of his poetic tributes, the King of Denmark, brother to the Queen and a visitor at this time to the English court.

In 1610 appeared in London the *Apologia* for the *Euphormionis Satyricon*, with which it was later reprinted as a third part. He here defends himself against the charge of

9*

libelling the Jesuits. In 1612 he published in
Paris a pamphlet entitled *Pietas,* in defence,
against King James's antagonist and his
subsequent patron Cardinal Bellarmine, of
his father's book *De Potestate Papae.* William Barclay, it may be noted, though anti-
papist was still more anti-Calvinist. Of this
book Casaubon wrote that Bellarmine *Suum
illum librum* . . . . *a Barclai filio* . . . *videbit
soricinia naenia confossiorem redditum* "will
soon see his book worse mangled than a
mouse in a trap by the younger Barclay." In
1614 appeared the *Icon Animorum,* later reprinted as a fourth part of the Satyricon,
with which it has no real relation, and last
of his London volumes, *Poemata: Libri Duo,*
a collection of his Latin verses (including
the best of *Sylvae).* In 1616, seeing no hope
of securing, as a Papist, a sure position at
court (and it was only on theological con-
troversies that James was prepared to spend
money) he left England, going first to Paris
and then, in the same year, at the invitation
of Pope Paul V, to Rome. He seems to have
retained King James's personal favour to the
last, receiving on his departure the King's
portrait in a golden locket set with jewels.

His invitation to Rome is said to have been the work of Gondomar, the former Spanish ambassador in London, but Cardinal Barberini (the Ibburranes of his *Argenis*) and his recent opponent Cardinal Bellarmine were his friends.

In return, we may suppose, for the Pope's hospitality, Barclay published at Rome in 1617 *Paraenesis ad Sectarios*, an ineffective contribution to religious controversy. He remained in Rome till his death, his last and most famous work *Argenis* appearing posthumously. He finished the book, says M. Dukas on the authority of a M. S., note in his own 1630 Elzevier edition, on 28th July, 1621, fell ill (of a fever) 1st August and died 12th August. This agrees with Winkelmann's account. He was buried near to the grave of Tasso in the graveyard of Saint Onofrio. The book which had been licensed by Pope Gregory XV and Louis XIII (to whom it was dedicated) was published by Nicolas Buon, under the care of Barclay's friend Peiresc, shortly afterwards.

He is said to have left behind him in M. S. a History *de Bello Sacro* (the capture of Jerusalem by the Franks) and fragments of a History of Europe.

§ 3.

Barclay was only $39\frac{1}{2}$ years old when he died and his widow, who though two years older than her husband survived him for 31 years, seems to have been properly proud of her husband. Bayle relates a story of how, observing that his tomb was in all respect similar to one which Cardinal Francis Barberini had made for his preceptor Bernard Guillaume, she sought to destroy it and failing in that attempt had the bust removed from it to her own house. " Her pride would not brook that her husband distinguished for his birth and yet more for his talent and his learning, should be made comparable with a wretched pedagogue ".

Barclay sprang into early fame with the first part of the *Satyricon* and must have been well known to the many scholars who were then in England. It is a little surprising therefore that he does not figure more prominently in the annals of King James's court. But the group whose names are mostly closely associated with the King and from whose entertainment he derived his reputation as the only monarch in all Europe who knew how to appreciate learning, that

group in which Launcelot Andrewes and
Casaubon are the most illustrious, devoted
its great parts on learning, as Grotius
complained, almost wholly to the study
of theology. It was indeed on this understanding and not from zeal for pure
scholarship that the King patronized them.
He desired the support of classical antiquity
for his own theories of the royal prerogative
and it was probably as the son of his
father, the Civil Lawyer and opponent of
the Jesuits, not as the commentator on
Statius or the writer of satirical romance
that James had welcomed him. These men
were assistants of James in his controversy
with Bellarmine and others and Barclay
would doubless have been more welcome
would he have written more in that line. But
though he defended his father's *De Potestate Papae*" he had thought fit to make
his own peace with the Jesuits for the dis-
respect shown them in his *Satyricon,* and his
verses and his *Icon Animorum* were of no
service to James's cause. With Casaubon
however, we know him to have been intimate.
He was with him on the expedition to Greenwich which preceded his death and as one
of the few French speakers at court he must

have been very welcome to that great
scholar who, though even in Scaliger's lifetime he knew more Greek than any man living, could not in his old age master the
English tongue.

There was another circle of scholars, of
perhaps greater fame, with whom Barclay
must have been acquainted, the antiquaries,
Cotton, Spelman, Camden and other friends
whose meetings the learned King suppress-
ed. But Barclay seems to have been even less
interested in archaeology than in theology,
and even pure scholarship was with him
only a study of his academic youth. A hundred years later he would have found his
congener in Swift rather than in Bentley.

Nevertheless these men knew and esteemed him. Grotius, who was in London for some
weeks in 1613, wrote on him a famous epigram (set beneath his portrait in several
Paris editions of *Argenis):*

> Gente Caledonius, Gallus natalibus. Hic est
> Romam Romano qui docet ore loqui.

which is not strictly accurate, for Lorraine,
where Barclay was born, was not then a
part of France.

Camden sent copies of *Icon Animorum* to
several of his foreign correspondents, and it

is interesting to find one of these writing
to Camden from Antwerp in June 1616 and
asking for a copy of this same book on behalf of "Rubenius celeberrimus pictor". The
same correspondent writes later in the year
"I hear Barclay is at Rome and is receiving
yearly 1000 gold pieces and his son 300".

§ 4.

We do not know very much about Barclay's character and opinions beyond what
we can infer from his writings. Winkelmann,
an early editor, describes him as "of graceful person and medium height, with mild
brow *(lene supercilium)*, soft gray eyes,
dark hair and a cheerful expression". For
the rest, we think of him as resembling
his own Nicopompus, a brilliant, versatile
cheerful personage, of moderate views,
easily apprehending both sides of any
question and equally ready to turn an elegy
on my lady's lapdog or deliver a weighty
dissertation on a point of civil government. "He was a man that from his infancy
loved learning; but who disdaining to be
nothing but a booke-man, had left the
Scholars very young, that in the courts of
Kings and Princes, he might serve his

prenticeship in publike affaires, his descent
and disposition fitting him for that kind of
life : wel esteemed of many Princes ". In
mentality he seems to stand on the thresh-
old of two ages. He is a Humanist of the
Renaissance in his scholarship, his depen-
dence on noble patronage, his freedom from
superstition tempered by reverence for the
old. We see in him a kinship to Machiavelli
and to Erasmus. On the other hand he is
a Jacobean man of letters, a contemporary of
Nash, of Jonson and of Shakespeare, with
an eye to the popular forms of art. Were it
not that it is written in Latin, the *Satyricon*
is as modern as *The Unfortunate Traveller,*
and *Argenis* is far more alive and contributes far more to the discussion of actual
problems than Lyly's *Euphues* or Sidney's
Arcadia. Goldsmith (another peripatetic
scholar) born a century and a half earlier
might have employed forms not so very
different from his.

We can well believe in the mildness and
cheerfulness of Barclay. His placable
character is reflected in his expressed
aversion* from duelling. Though continually
satirizing he never seems to have given

* See the Dedication, to Louis XIII, of his *Argenis.*

serious offence. He found it necessary to write a defence of his alleged attacks on the Jesuits (under the name of *Acignii*) in the *Satyricon,* but that apparently ended the controversy and they seem to have displayed no hostility to him subsequently. Though a friend of James I and even in *Argenis* an opposer of all extreme clerical claims he enjoyed to the end the patronage of Cardinals and Popes, and though he never abandoned the Roman church he seems never to have been objected to on that score by Protestants or Anglicans. His final withdrawal from England seems to have been due to no personal hostility.

§ 5.

The *Euphormionis Satyricon* has never yet found an English translator, though Thomas May made a version of the *Icon Animorum* which appears as its fourth book, under the title of *A Mirror of Minds,* published in 1631 (?). Of the *Argenis* there are two early translations and one very much later. The early translators were Sir Robert Le Grys, Knight, and Kingsmill Long, Gent. Their successor, in the 18th century, was Miss Clara Reeve, author of a number of

novels of one of which the name at any
rate has still some fame — *The Old English
Baron* (1777). Of the two early translators
hardly anything besides the authorship
of these versions is known. No less a person
than Ben Jonson appears on the records of
the Stationers' Company as having register-
ed a translation in 1621, that is the very year
of the book's appearance in Paris. But there
is no further trace of his undertaking and
since Le Grys's edition was "upon his Majesty's Command", it seems likely that Ben,
who about that time was busy writing court
masques, was instructed to do the work by
the learned King but turned it over to
another. The verses are by Thomas May and
had already appeared in Kingsmill Long's
translation.

Le Grys' version, a quarto volume, was
first published in 1628. This is the date correctly given by Sir David Dalrymple in his
'Sketch of the Life of John Barclay', but
later bibliographers write 1629. I have seen
only one copy bearing the earlier date, but
the 1629 edition, which is that commonly
found, differs in no other particular that I
have discerned than the substitution of 9
for 8. The title-page runs:

JOHN
BARCLAY
HIS
ARGENIS
TRANSLATED OUT
OF LATINE INTO
ENGLISH:
THE PROSE VPON HIS

Majesties Command:

By Sir ROBERT LE GRYS, Knight:

And the Verses by Thomas May, Esquire.

With a Clauis annexed to it for the satisfaction of the

Reader, and helping him to understand, what persons were by

the Author intended, under the fained Names imposed

by him vpon them:

And published by his Maiesties Command.

LONDON,

Printed by Felix Kyngston for Richard Meighen and

Henry Seile. 1628.

The dedication is to the King and makes one wonder how the King or Ben Jonson came to light on Sir Robert. But he is not so ignorant of Latin as he professes to be. With or without a knowledge of Latin grammar he could evidently construe pretty correctly. On the whole, indeed he is a better Latinist than his rival Long, but he

makes one amusing error. Argenis, records
that Selenissa was wont to beguile her se-
clusion by practising archery. She would exercise her arm-muscles with a bow, *" facili arcu
fatigabat lacertos"*. Which Le Grys delight-
fully renders, "There with her little Bow
she troubled the Lizartes". I fear the fault
is wholly Le Grys', for no text that I have
seen reads "lacertas". There seems to be no
reprint of this version subsequent to 1629.

The other version, Kingsmill Long's,
though it must yield place to the Royal
Command, can claim the priority in time. It
was published in folio in 1625. It was printed by G. P. for Henry Seile. Nothing is said
about the verses but they are identical with
those given by Le Grys. Of this a second
edition was printed "for Henry Seile,
at the signs of the Tygres Head in Fleet
Street neare the Conduit" in 1636. This is a
quarto volume and contains a number of
engravings. It is in the words of the title
page "The Second Edition, Beautified with
Pictures." Long had now risen to the state
of "Esquire."

Neither of the two translations is among
the very best specimens in this kind of
Tudor and Jacobean prose. Le Grys is rather

the more vigorous and his choice of words is good. He is not afraid of the vernacular. But his constructions are a little clumsy, repeating too plainly the Latin form, and the rhythm, the glory of the prose of the age, is poor. Long's is a more fluent version but rather characterless. Miss Clara Reeve, the third translator, remarks: "There is in the style [of Le Grys] a simplicity that is pleasing and even respectable, while in the latter there is a kind of affectation that in some places rises to bombast and others descends to vulgarity." Her own version, a plain, insipid performance, was published in 4 octavo volumes in 1772 under the title of "The Phoenix, or the History of Polyarchus and Argenis."

In the *Cambridge History of English Literature*, Professor Bensley, who contributes an admirable account of Barclay, notices an 18th century abridgment by the Rev. John Jacobs, entitled "The Adventures of Poliarchus and Argenis".

These are the only English editions of this famous book, and only two editions of the Latin text have ever been printed in this country, one by Thomas Huggins, at Oxford, in 1634, another by J. Hayes, at Cambridge in 1673 and 1674. But on the Continent it has had a much more eventful career. Three French versions had appeared before Long's English one and they were many times reprinted. The earliest was one by P. Marcassus in 1622, reprinted in 1626. In 1623 appeared a *traduction nouvelle* usually ascribed to P. du Ryer (or Durier), but claimed by Dr. Schmid for one N. Guibert, which achieved greater popularity and was reprinted eight times in the next twenty years. A third version by Coffeteau, Bishop of Marseilles was published in 1624 and three times reprinted in twenty years, a fourth by P. de Lungue appeared in 1628 and was reprinted in 1662; a fifth by the Abbé Josse appeared in 1632 and was reprinted three times, in 1634, 1654 and 1664; the sixth and last version by Savin appeared in 1671.

Translations into all the principal languages of Europe were also made. Dr. Schmid records early versions in Spanish (first published in 1626), Italian (1629 and 1630), German (in 1626, 1631 and four other early versions; besides which a new one was printed as late as 1891), Dutch (1643), Polish (1697), and Icelandic (1694). In the 18th Century the process continued. Versions

appeared in Swedish (1740), in Danish
(1746), in Russian (1751), in Magyar (1792).

Moreover the Latin editions were no less
numerous. The book was published at Stras-
burg and at Frankfort in the year following
its original appearance and several times reprinted within a decade. At Paris itself a
second Latin edition came from Buon's press
in 1623, with a portrait of the author by D.
du Monotier, engraved by C. Mellar. The third
Paris edition is of 1623, and others followed in 1624, 1625, 1632, 1633, 1638, 1639 and
1643. Meanwhile the famous *officina Elzevi-
riana* had taken it in hand and published
many editions, the first, with a *clavis,* in
1627, the second, with a *discursus de auctore*
in 1630. In 1659 what purports to be a two
volume edition appeared edited by Bugnot,
ex officina Hackiana, of Leyden and Rotter-
dam. In reality the first volume is an annotated edition of Barclay's work; the second
volume is a continuation or imitation by
Bugnot entitled *Archombrotus & Theopompus.* Theopompus is the Dauphin, whom, in
dedicating to him the second part of his own
volume, he extols as the ideal Prince, resembling *inter alios* Antony of Guevara's
Marcus Aurelius. Continuations of this kind

10

were common, the earliest being one by
M. A. M. de Mouchambert, published in Paris
as early as 1625.

Another annotated edition was put forth
as late as 1768, at Nuremberg, by Winkelmann. This is described as the 17th edition
of the work, but in all Dr. Schmid enumerated 54 distinct impressions, all but 8 of them
being of the 17th century.

The collation of the Latin texts is a
labour I have not undertaken, but I observe
that the Elzevier edition of 1627 and all the
subsequent editions that I have seen contain
in at least one place considerable passages
which are not in the early Paris editions and
are consequently not in the early French or
English versions.

§ 6.

Argenis is in the direct line of descent
from the Greek novel—from the Aethiopian
Histories of Heliodorus, that shadow auth-
or of whom legend, beautifully but un-
warrantably, relates that he was a bishop
and preferred, the choice being imposed on
him, the fame of his book to the retention of
his See. In the *Aethiopica* you already get
the ingredients of Barclay's romance: the

child—lost, stolen or strayed—restored after long years to its noble parents; the disguised sex; the robbers—pirates or bandits; battle and murder; many voyagings; much loving with its accompaniments of jealousies, rivalries, misunderstandings and impassioned protestations: and those inheritances from comedy, the trusty retainer and the false, intriguing hand-maid. All these things you have in Barclay, blended with as little probability as ever. But Barclay handles them with a good deal of structural skill. There are not quite so many narratives let in to the main fabric and those there are do as a rule help to carry the story or explain a mystery in the matter in hand. Moreover Barclay really does contrive to excite your curiosity as to how the whole imbroglio is to end. He has two heroes, Polyarchus and Archombrotus, and though Archombrotus is allowed to lapse into a disloyalty to his friend that disqualifies him as a Hero of Romance, yet his fall is not irretrievable and the completely happy ending requires that he shall be plausibly recompensed for the inevitable loss—since two men cannot win her of Argenis. The solution of their difficulty is concealed with no little skill. The

10*

introduction of the poet Nicopompus, with his frequent snatches of verse, is a novelty. Unfortunately the verses, neatly turned pieces of Latinity, are at their best merely ingenious and well-phrased and in their English dress wear always an academic and ceremonial air. But Nicopompus was a main figure in what was unquestionably the most distinguishing feature of the book—its discourses and dialogues on matters of state-craft. To these and to the belief that the whole book was a political allegory it owed its highest fame. It was, we may be sure, for its discourses on the advantage of a centralised authority and kindred topics that the great Richelieu valued it as he is said to have done, having it continually in his hands. It was for these and not for its romantic qualities that King James ordered it to be translated into English, that his unlearned subjects might learn properly to estimate the value of monarchy of which in hereditary and constitutional form Barclay is a strong and wise advocate. So late as 1674 an Erfurt professor thought it worth while publishing a collection of political excerpts from the book.

Yet one is tempted, on reading Barclay's books, to fancy that what he really wanted to do was to write novels. But novel-writing was scarcely a more reputable occupation than play-writing. In both modes only the pastoral could claim really genteel sponsorship. And even into the pastoral the serious minded felt it necessary to put an element of political allegory, witness the example of Lyly not only in his rather dull and artificial *Euphues,* but in his comedies, those brilliant and beautiful pieces of poetic wit —poetic, in the highest sense, even in their prose.

And Barclay was a literary soldier of fortune—equipped by his father with a great deal of learning and true Scottish enterprise, and sent forth to open the oyster of the world with his pen. Kings—and learned ones at that—were to be his patrons and he could not suffer himself to indulge without disguise his taste for Romance. So in his first 'novel' *Euphormionis Satyricon,* the scholarly and clerical element is stressed. His wandering hero is no common footboy, like Jack Wilton in Nash's famous *Unfortunate Traveller,* but a scholar, the prototype being, it is supposed, in the first

part his father, the Professor of Laws, in
the second his precocious self, and both ab-
sorb the sack of pure adventure in many
solid loaves of philosophic disputation. The
two subsequent parts are still more serious :
the third being an elaborate defence of himself against the charge of libelling the
Jesuits, the fourth the interesting *Eikon
Animorum,* the *Mirror of Souls,* a series of
essays on the national characteristics of the
nations of Europe. The fifth part is, by
general agreement, spurious.

This first novel was dedicated to the
Scholar King, James Stuart, his second to the
young King of France, Louis XIII, and the
chosen theme this time is *la haute Politique.*
It was written for the great and for the
learned and it was not to be thought of that
such persons could be interested by a mere
idle tale of robbers and shipwrecks and feign-
ed love-makings. Nevertheless there are
plenty of these things there. One wonders,
indeed, whether this is really a pill coated
with sugar, or a toothsome sweet labelled
Pilula Medicinalis. It is interesting to note
that Kingsmill Long when he came to translate it into the vernacular, though he praises it for its wise and political discourses

and insists on the profit to the Reader, yet
sets on the title-page a sub-title "The Loves
of Polyarchus and Argenis." On the other
hand the keys which were soon added to all
editions show that the allegory contributed
largely to the popularity of the story.

To us however the allegorical truth that
may or may not underlie the fiction is
of far less interest. The book, in whole and
in particulars, is too little capable of exact
interpretation to be of any value as an historical document. As a shrewd contemporary estimate of political institutions it has
value: as a record of happenings is has none.
The man in the street likes to see contemporary events, particularly scandalous ones,
hinted at, and notable figures of the hour depicted. But they get no such knowledge from
such portraiture, and this kind of writing is
journalism rather than literature and not
even such journalism as furnishes documents for the historian of subsequent generations, for Barclay cannot be said to give
any intimate impressions of his contemporary models or to make them live for us in
any degree. Archombrotus decidedly has
character; the subtleness with which he is
differentiated from Polyarchus is undeni-

able. But in neither Archombrotus nor Polyarchus do we seem to see the living linea-
ments of their supposed original, Henry of
Navarre.

As always in such cases, the editors have
been inclined to press the analogies too far,
but Barclay's own theory of the political
novel, set forth by Nicopompus, makes it
certain that he had an allegorical intention.
Le Grys' *Key* shows at any rate what the
contemporary critics made of it.

The most interesting identifications are
of the characters who take part not so much
in the romance as in the political dialogues.
Of these Nicopompus is Barclay himself;
Ibburranes, Cardinal Barberini (alias Pope
Urban); Dunalbius, Cardinal Ubaldini, the
Papal Legate in England; Hieroleander, Hie-
ronymus Leander. Usimulca, leader of the
Hyperaphanii, is, of course, Calvin. Professor Bensley suggests Sillery for Cleobulus,
but the old Clavis makers confidently de-
clare him to be Villeroy.

As to the sources of the book little need
be said. Much of Barclay's material is the
common stuff of all romances, and he draws
freely, too, on the Roman historians—
notably Tacitus and Polybius. A more re-

markable borrowing is from the Danish *Saxo Grammaticus,* who otherwise touches our literature mainly through his evidence as to the historical element in *Beowulf.* To him M. Dupont traces the whole episode of Theocrine.

§ 7.

There is certainly more varied and elaborate characterization in Barclay than in the vast majority of contemporary novels in the vernaculars. Cervantes is on another plane and the drama was far more highly developed in this as in most other respects. But though there may be elsewhere flashes of acuter insight into human character and what is perhaps more important, of greater vividness in its representation, these are only in scattered passages and on a small scale. The longer and more famous novels, such as Lyly's *Euphues* and Sidney's *Arcadia,* to mention only the English examples, give no such definite and distinctly charactered portraits as the worthy, but rather ineffective Meleander, the spirited Argenis, most faithful in love without being romantically absurd, the two subtly contrasted gallants, Archombrotus and Polyarchus, the dashing ' villain ', who

is yet a very serviceable person, Radiroba-
nes, the plausible and disloyal Lycogenes.
Even the quite minor figures have a certain
air of reality, though most of them are of a
type common to all books of this kind—Selenissa the intriguing lady-in-waiting, Hyanisbe, the ' long lost ' mother, and the council-
lors and courtiers, though in the main they
exist to be interlocutors in Barclay's political dialogues, have yet a consistent individuality and now and then are lighted up with
touches of personal and even humorous
triviality ; Nicopompus, for example, who
disarms criticism by attributing his verses
to his small son, an incident which reminds
us of the alleged paternal authorship of
Euphormionis Satyricon. There is humour
too in such touches as the hoarseness of the
herald who had to read Hyanisbe's " exceed-
ing long epistle ".

The whole story is, like so many books in
those " spacious " days, longer than modern
taste entirely relishes, but the plot, in spite
of the many interpolated narratives, is
closely and skilfully connected. The interpolations are not irrelevant tales but pieces
of the history (of which the action begins,
in the most approved modern fashion, near

the crisis) told retrospectively, and of necessity for the elucidation of the whole. How cunningly devised a situation is that at the end of the book when Polyarchus, being induced by Hyanisbe to lay aside his natural hostility towards Archombrotus, is brought before Meleander only, as he thinks, to be mocked by the sight of that King, after reading Hyanisbe's letter, embracing Archombrotus and persuading Argenis even to do the same. Poliarchus lays hand on sword and for a moment vows vengeance on the faithless lady love. Yet two pages later all is satisfactorily explained and Argenis is his bashful betrothed and Archombrotus his most affectionate friend.

In no age has the book lacked its admirers. Cowley thought it the finest Romance ever written. Cowper wrote of it in a letter to S. Rose: "It is interesting in a high degree; either in incident that can be imagined, full of surprise, which the reader never forestalls, and yet free from all entanglement and confusion. The style, too, appears to me such as would not dishonour Tacitus himself". The praise of Coleridge is to be found in his brother-in-law, Southey's copy of the book (in the Grenville Library). Hallam

places Barclay second only to Cervantes. On
the continent Richelieu and Leibnitz were
among its devoted readers. No common book
could win praise from critics of such different stamps.

§ 8.

As a Latinist Barclay was highly, and
even extravagantly, eulogized by his own
contemporaries, notably by Hugo Grotius,
and their praise has been echoed by Coleridge, Hallam and other modern critics.
Against these, however, must be set the
adverse judgment of Scaliger who says he
could 'scarcely read six pages of it.' But
Scaliger was a very censorious person who
disliked the English and judged Latin by the
best classical standard. Barclay, who used
Latin as a living tongue, never aimed at the
Ciceronian classicism that became the pure
scholar. Also, as he seems not to have been a
Greek scholar Scaliger would not regard him
as 'doctissimus.' In contemporary romance
Scaliger probably took no interest at all. If
one whose reading in later Latin is narrow
may venture an opinion, these eulogies are
not undeserved. Barclay avoids barbarisms
on the one hand and classical clichés (to

which the modern Latinist, like the Babu writer of English, is most prone) on the other. He writes clearly and pithily and achieves at times an almost Tacitean cadence and a little of the impressive pregnancy of Tacitean utterance. Coleridge declared that he was to be preferred to Livy, Hallam, whose praises are more modified, finds him more akin to Petronius Arbiter, with whom of course his subject matter more naturally links him. His vocabulary is as pure as can be desired in a writer who uses Latin as a living tongue and not as an instrument of academic fame. Neither his diction nor his syntax would always please the modern schoolmaster, but Barclay, it must be remembered, was constantly reading the Latin of all periods, and speaking it in common life, and was not seeking to reproduce faithfully the idiom of the " golden " age. He uses, too, a more loosely figurative, a more " coloured " style than the best Roman writers have cared for.

But what matters it now how he wrote. He rejected the English tongue, and was not fortunate enough to find a translator of genius. The third centenary of *Argenis'* birth heard no echo of his former fame.

ABRAHAM COWLEY.

§ 1.

'WHO now reads Cowley?' asked Pope, some three-quarters of a century after Cowley's death:

> Who now reads Cowley? if he pleases yet,
> His moral pleases not his pointed wit;
> Forget his epic, nay, Pindaric art;
> But still I love the language of his heart.
> *(Epistle to Augustus, 11. 75—8.)*

But Cowley's fame was not dead, as Pope proceeds to testify. 'Yet surely, surely these were famous men,'

> In all debates where critics bear a part
> Not one but nods and talks of Johnson's art,
> Of Shakespeare's nature, and of Cowley's wit.
> *(ibid. 11. 81—3.)*

Half a century later this state of things had not altered. Johnson (Samuel, this time, not Ben) and his syndicate of booksellers take Cowley as the starting point for their survey of the field of modern English poetry. Johnson treats Cowley as the last and the

highest product of the 'metaphysical school',
whose beginnings he finds, in England, in
Jonson and Donne; and though Johnson had
little liking for that mode of writing, he is
according Cowley very high rank among
English poets. He speaks of Cowley's 'Pin-
darism' as having 'prevailed about half a
century', which would date its decline at the
period of Pope's rise, but his subsequent
censure of the *Davideis* suggests that Cowley was still held in high regard: 'there are
not many examples of so great a work, produced by an author *generally read, and generally praised,* that has crept through the
century with so little regard'.

Pass on another century, and the fading
memory of Cowley's fame is wholly gone. In
1880, Mr. T. H. Ward could write: 'except for
a few students like Lamb and Sir Egerton
Brydges, Cowley's verse is in this century
unread and unreadable. Not even the antiquarian curiosity of an age which reprints
Brathwaite and Crowne has yet availed to
present him in a new edition.' This last re-
proach Cowley's own University of Cambridge has since removed, and modern criticism, including Mr. Ward's, has in some
small degree restored his reputation; but he

still lacks readers, though the present age
has more sympathy than any since their own
day with his more mystical contemporaries
and forerunners, and his own style of verse
should prove far more to its liking than to
that of Pope or Johnson, coupleteers both.

§ 2.

Cowley's life, had it ever been written
at full length, should have proved more interesting than most poets', for he lived in stirring times and played an active and eventful
part. But I do not think increased knowledge
of the man would help us to any better appre-
ciation of his poetry. For that is only in a
very general way based on his experience ;
rather it reflects the play of his fancy and
his intelligence. It displays learning more
than wisdom, quick perception of the incon-
gruities and resemblances in ideas and things
rather than a 'philosophy of life' or any
burning passions. He was, in the jargon of
the literary historian, a wit, not a seer, or
even a singer.

Cowley was of humble birth, but bred
among the aristocracy and consequently
perhaps a little too apt to overvalue that intellectual facility which had won him his

11

elevation in station. He was born in 1618, the
posthumous son of a London stationer (Johnson says a grocer), and at a very early age
was infected with the virus of poetry by
reading Spenser's *Faery Queen,* a copy of
which lay in his mother's parlour. He was
sent to Westminster School, the nursery of
Ben Jonson and several of his famous ' sons ',
then presided over by the learned William
Camden. He learned with fatal facility and
failed to get elected, at his first attempt, to a
scholarship at Trinity, Cambridge, although
both in English and in Latin he had already
made himself known as a poet. He was however duly elected in the following year, 1637,
and proceeded to Cambridge,* ' where by the
Progress and Continuance of his Wit, it
appeared that two things were joined in it
which seldom meet together, that it was both
early and lasting.'

He was still at Cambridge, now Fellow of
Trinity and a noted wit, when the Civil War
broke out, and he removed from Puritanical
East Anglia to Laudian Oxford, where he
attracted the favourable notice of the King
and Queen, and of the excellent and talented
Lucius Carey, Lord Falkland. From now on-

---

* According to Johnson he went to Cambridge in 1636.

wards he was in royal employment, being particularly charged with coding and decoding the royal correspondence. When the King's fortunes were in eclipse, Cowley went to Paris with the Queen† and his immediate chief Lord St. Albans. He returned to England in 1656 on some kind of secret service and was seized by the Commonwealth authorities, but released on bail, when he turned Doctor of Physic§ and complied with the *de facto* government till Cromwell's death. He then again went to France, with the consent, it is presumed, of his surety and without any molestation from the now tottering government. At the Restoration he returned to London and court attendance; but Charles, though very complimentary towards him, was in no hurry to afford him any material comfort. At length, through the good offices of St. Albans and of Buckingham, he obtained a lease of certain lands of the Queen at Chertsey, to which neighbourhood he retired in 1665. Here he died, at the

---

† To this the portrait of Cowley in the N. P. G. assigns the date 1646. It also states that he had been entered at St. John's College, Oxford.

§ He was subsequently one of the original members of the Royal Society.

Porch House, in 1667, being not yet forty-nine years old.

The bulk of Cowley's work is not great, though he began to write at the tenderest possible age, his *Poeticall Blossomes,* including *Constantia and Philetus* and *The Tragicall History of Piramus and Thisbe* (which he claimed to have written at ten years of age), being certainly in print by 1633. While he was still ' Kings Scholler in Westminster Schoole ' he wrote a pastoral comedy, *Loves Riddle;* and at Cambridge a Latin comedy, and he had a comedy, *The Guardian,* acted there before Prince Charles. He wrote also many poetic pieces during these and the following years, which were collected into a folio volume in 1656 under the four headings, I. Miscellanies; II. The Mistress; III. Pindarique Odes; IV. Davideis. This volume includes the bulk of Cowley's English work, but after the restoration he published his longest Latin poem, *Of Plants,* a new version of his early comedy under the title of *Cutter of Coleman Street* (not *THE Cutter),* and a few *Odes* and *Verses upon several occasions;* all of which, together with the contents of the 1656 folio, were collected after his death into another folio, wherein also first appeared

those admirable examples of the 'language
of his heart', *Several Discourses by way of
Essays, in Verse and Prose.* This collection,
edited by Thomas Sprat, appeared in 1668
and was often reprinted in two volumes. A
third volume, containing the rejected early
work, appeared in 1681.

§ 3.

There is surprisingly little influence of
Cowley's varied and stirring experiences to
be traced in this body of verse. Much of it,
being occasional, does, of course, contain direct references to historical events and personages; but on the manner of the verse and
the personality of the writer these happenings wrought little or no change. The man
and his art seem to slip through these eventful years, reflecting them indeed from their
surface, but essentially untouched. Cowley
indeed claims that he never had any natural
taste for a court or public life, and that his
literary studies and creative works were a
thing apart, and when, 'turn'd beyond forty',
he withdrew from the business of the world,
he was at last following his true bent.

Westminster has always been a nursery for
poets, teaching them, as she did Cowper, 'to

set a distich into six and five', in English as well in Latin, and Cowley, 'made irremediably a poet' before he was twelve by the infection of Spenser's tinkling rhyme and dancing numbers (the phrase is Cowley's), is a very type of the poet made as well as born. He was a born poet beyond a doubt : but he suffered from precocity and perhaps from excess of instruction. He acquired a manner very early, before he had any matter to employ it on, and his facility later led much of his best work to spend itself in wide, shallow, ineffective rivulets of verse instead of gathering head and cutting deep and solid-bottomed channels.

This manner of his Johnson has labelled, for all time, 'metaphysical'. He does not define metaphysical, and the meaning it here bears is not its philosophical one ; but the examples he quotes from Cowley himself and from Donne make clear what he means by it. Lewis Carroll might have explained it as a portmanteau word, a blend of 'metaphorical' and 'physical'. With greater etymological truth we might define it as 'confusing natures', for the chief characteristic of the style is an abundance and elaboration of metaphors, drawn mostly from the physical

sciences, which, at the instigation of Bacon
and his disciples, were being much studied
in literary circles. 'The most heterogeneous
ideas,' says Johnson, 'are yoked together ;
nature and art are ransacked for illustra-
tions, comparisons, and allusions.'

Donne is today a poet who receives much
attention ; and George Herbert and the
mystics—Vaughan, Crashaw, Traherne—with
their attemps to transcend reason and the
senses and get at the essence of the object,
if less written of, are nearer akin than any
other group of poets to more than one type
of contemporary poetry. But Cowley, though
Johnson was perfectly right in setting him
in this company, has marked differences, and
it is to these distinctive qualities he owes his
contemporary popularity and his later
oblivion.

§ 4.

The poet of wide contemporary reputation, if he is not simply a bad poet or a
people's poet of the ballad-making type, must
do one of two things : he must either take an
existing form, which is known to be approved by the critics, and exploit it by making it
more attractive to the general reader, in

theme and in style, or he must take a popular
subject and treat it skilfully in any easily
read metre. Thus à tolerably good poet sim-
plifying and polishing his predecessors' style
may come to be thought a very good one; a
good story-teller writing in passably good
verse may be hailed as a great poet. Scott
may serve as an example of the second, Cowley of the first.

Cowley is an easy poet : he wrote with ease,
he can be read with ease. He is seldom obscure, discordant, or dull. His predecessors,
particularly from the worldly-wise-man's
point of view, were frequently all three. He
was not quite as 'correct' as Waller, so that
even Dryden thought him a great poet but
not a good writer, and Pope, who had abnormal gifts in this direction, quite eclipsed him.
Yet the most superior persons would have to
admit that he was learned and gifted with all
the recognized poetic qualities of the day—
a day which had lost sight of the true merits
of Shakespeare, and as yet knew not its own
particular star, Milton. Here was a poet of
the widest and deepest learning who yet
wrote Anacreontics and verses to his mistress (apparently a quite apocryphal person); who wrote of Mr. Hobbes's philosophy

so that any man might understand his meaning and enjoy his rhythmic verse; who translated Pindar into easy and mellifluous English ; who even wrote a sacred epic which made David and Jonathan and Michal as interesting as that popular hero, Fairfax's (and Tasso's) Godfrey of Bulloigne.

Why then, it will be asked, if Cowley really possessed these poetic gifts, did he so quickly lose his reputation and still more quickly his readers? Because, borne on the crest of the metaphysical wave, he went with the fashion too far, into the trough of the wave, so that it was clear, to more reflecting readers and to a generation not bred to the taste for it, that the metaphysical manner had degenerated into a mere fashionable device and was not, as it had been on the lips of its first users, a real help to the expression of subtle and hardly comprehended ideas. And, further, because, so far as concerned his movement towards clarity and fluency, others very soon carried it further, particularly with respect to the metre in which Cowley wrote his epic, but not, in bulk, anything else, the fivefooted couplet. Herein Waller, a very empty poet, had achieved greater technical success, and after him Dryden and then Pope made Cowley's verse seem rough and unskilful. Of the Ode, though he may have misused the name of Pindar, he remained a master, but the couplet, as we know, swallowed up all its brethren, not even Dryden's magnificent work sufficing to keep this one alive. Johnson thought little of this part of Cowley's poetry, but Johnson was equally scornful of Gray's *Odes,* and would probably not have valued Words-worth's.

There remain the Essays, of which the prose portion has of late years been often reprinted, so that Cowley has oddly enough been in greater esteem as a prose writer than as a poet. Of the verse 'essays', some approximate to the style of the Poems on Various Occasions, some are in that simple gnomic vein which the coupleteers now and then affected, notably, for example, Pope in his 'Happy the man whose wish and care A few paternal acres bound.' It is to these probably that Pope refers with so much affection in the familiar lines I have already quoted. But it was not on these that Cowley's original reputation rested, and though possibly his best they are certainly not his most characteristic work.

§ 5.

'Wit' is the quality which has always been associated with Cowley's name, and the association is justified; but Cowley's 'wit' needs to be distinguished from the later, much better known Popian variety, 'what oft was thought, but ne'er so well expressed'. Ingenuity and novelty are here more sought after than that common sense and polished simplicity at which the couplet writers aimed.

Cowley himself wrote an ode 'Of Wit'. We learn from it several things which wit, in the author's view, is not:

'T is not in Tale, 't is not in Jest,
Admired with Laughter at a Feast
Nor florid Talk . . . .

.   .   .   .

'T is not to force some lifeless Verses meet
With their five gouty Feet.

.   .   .   .

'T is not when two like Words make up one Noise
Jests for Dutch Men and English Boys
In which who finds out Wit, the same may see
In An'grams and Acrostiques Poetry.

.   .   .   .

'T is not such Lines as almost crack the Stage,
When Bajazet begins to rage.
Nor a tall Met'phor in the Bombast way,
Nor the dry Chips of short lung'd Seneca
Nor upon all things to obtrude,
And force some odd similitude.

' What is it then? ', he asks, and, alas, we are not greatly enlightened by his own answer :

> In a true Piece of Wit all things must be,
> Yet all things there agree.

This is not a satisfactory definition, even though he adds the ' odd similitude ',

> As in the ark. . . . .

Yet Cowley's meaning can be partly guessed at and a closer examination of his own practice will make it clearer.

This ode is one of the earlier pieces printed under the heading of *Miscellanies,* of which Cowley speaks disparagingly as having ' no extraordinary virtue '. There is one piece here that has been honoured by inclusion in many anthologies, *The Chronicle,* a list of the fair ones who had in succession possessed the poet's heart, and the lines on the death of his friend the poet Crashaw are interesting and skilful, though not equal to his elegy *On the Death of Mr. William Harvey,* a really moving poem and not unworthy to be mentioned in the same breath with Milton's and with Matthew Arnold's similar poems. But this collection as a whole would not have won a mature poet any high reputation and, what is more, there is not a great deal that would make the reader remark particularly on Cowley's wit. The similes are many, but not extravagant and not sustained in the way Herbert's, for example, are. It is not at all easy to classify Cowley at this time. His earliest master in poetry was Spenser, but there is not a great deal of Spenserian influence evident, either in matter or in manner, even in those early *Poetical Blossomes.* As becomes a Westminster poet he seems to owe more to Jonson, in his commemorative and complimentary vein, and to the Romans, notably Horace and Ovid, and but that he was in France we should expect to find him among the fifty three poets (and one publisher) who lamented the death of that illustrious ' son of Ben ', Will Cartwright. It is only here and there that Cowley touches the note of true poetry, but he shows a rather remarkable faculty for avoiding the extremes of fatuous rhetoric in which even the young Dryden indulged.

In the second section of his '56 folio, *The Mistress,* the conceits are greater and more. The testimony of credible witnesses can be brought to prove the insincerity of these amorous pieces, and the internal evidence

agrees therewith. But the verse is bright and
facile; no one before the Queen Anne men
wrote better than he such elegant jingles as
this :

> I know 't is sordid and 't is low
> (All this as well as you I know)
> Which I so hotly now pursue:
> (I know all this as well as you).

While this is in the century's best lyric
manner :

> Love in her Sunny Eyes does basking play;
>   Love walks the pleasant Mazes of her Hair,
> Love does on both her Lips for ever stray
>   And sows and reaps a thousand Kisses there.

The Spring is a charming and most skilful
piece of prettiness and wit, and *The Wish* is
a very graceful expression of the modest
ambitions which, in spite of the cynicism of
the very urban Doctor Johnson, he sincerely
fostered and in the end gladly achieved :

> Ah, yet, e'er I descend to th' Grave,
> May I a small House, and large Garden have!
> And a few Friends, and many Books, both true,
>   Both wise, and both delightful too!
> Oh, Fountains, when in you shall I
> Myself, eas'd of unpeaceful Thoughts, espy?
> Oh Fields! Oh Woods! When, when shall I be made
>   The happy Tenant of your Shade?

The Mistress won great popularity, which
probably led Cowley to stress the element of

conceit in his subsequent poetry. The *Pindaric Odes* which follow possess admirable qualities,—moving language, melody and imagery. Few poets have ever written in such a coloured style yet with such lucidity and directness. The seventh stanza of the second ode will furnish a brief example; the subject is the story of the infant Hercules strangling the serpents:

Some of th' amazed Women dropp'd down dead
  With Fear, some wildly fled
About the Room, some into Corners crept,
  Where silently they shook and wept.
All naked from her Bed the passionate Mother leap'd
  To save or perish with her Child,
She trembled and she cried, the mighty Infant smil'd
  The mighty Infant seem'd well pleas'd
  At his gay gilded Foes.
And as their spotted necks up to the Cradle rose,
With his young warlike Hands on both he seized;
  In vain they rag'd, in vain they hist,
  In vain their armed Tails they twist,
And angry Circles cast about,
Black Blood, and fiery Breath, and pois'nous Soul he
               squeezes out.

To object to these Odes that they do not really represent the prosody of Pindar is little to the point. The first two are indeed translations, but elsewhere an unjustified name should not be allowed to damn vigorous and full-blooded verse. At times the rhyme and the rhythm are too much in the manner of

the Comic poet, but at least these odes are
never, as most of their successors have been,
turgid and full of air. They will suffer the
pricking of a hole or two in them without
deflation. In the third ode (an Horatian one)
he uses of Pindar words that are not inapplic-
able to himself :

> Whether at Pisa's Race he please
> To carve in polish'd verse the Conqu'rors Images,
> Whether the swift, the skilful, or the strong,
> Be crowned in his nimble, artful, vigorous Song,
> Whether some brave young man's untimely Fate
> In words worth dying for he celebrate,
>
> . . . .
> The Grave can but the Dross of him devour,
> So small is Death's, so great the Poet's Power.

The ode called *The Resurrection* is a good
example of what Cowley calls the ' enthusias-
tical manner,' and *To Mr. Hobs* a panegyric
not only well-phrased but, what is rarer in
panegyrics, well-reasoned. Indeed hardly one
of the Odes fails to impress as being the
work of a man not merely of exceptional
learning and metrical skill, but of real intellect and vision.

§ 6.

The Davideis has had few admirers and
today, I suppose, has no readers. Nobody
reads epics, good or bad, and the story of

David is much more heroically told in the Book of Samuel. The poem was, we are told, to have had twelve books, because the Aeneid had. For a similar bad reason it was to have ended before David acquired his kingdom. Yet in spite of all this and of a notable inferiority of the whole to the parts, the poem has its merits. The verse never lapses into mere connecting links between episodes. There are many bad lines and passages, but hardly any flat ones. Cowley always, here and elsewhere, has something to say. It may be the wrong thing, but it is never dull prosing, nor yet mere sound and fury. And it is no small feat to have written even four books of an epic and kept clear of that Scylla and that Charybdis.

The *Davideis,* though printed as the third section of the Works, is supposed to have been written at Cambridge. The fourth or fifth sections really were the last composed and represent Cowley's art at its maturest and best. Leigh, one of the contributors to Cartwright's posthumous *Collected Poems,* had written in 1651,

Give us what Cowley's later years brought forth.
His Mistresse shows he was a wit by birth;

suggesting with sound judgment that a

12

less exuberant and more thoughtful maturity
would bring added qualities to Cowley's
muse. In these pieces, if Cowley's head is
still among the clouds of fancy, his feet are
firmly planted on the ground of personal experience. The ' occasions ' of the first section
supply substance for Cowley's playful or
phantastic humour : in the second, he is giving utterance to the ripe judgment of a re-
flective and well stored mind. *The Complaint*,
in which Cowley laments his lack of advancement, abounds in similes, but of a most appro-
priate kind. There is true wit, in the modern
as well as in the metaphysical sense of the
word, in the fourth stanza :

> As a fair morning of the blessed spring,
>   After a tedious stormy night,
> Such was the glorious entry of our king
> Enriching moisture dropp'd on every thing.
> Plenty he sow'd below, and cast about him light.
>   But then (alas) to thee alone,
> One of old Gideon's Mirsacles was shown.
> For ev'ry Tree, and ev'ry Herb around,
>   With Pearly Dew was crown'd,
> And upon all the quickened Ground,
> The fruitful Seed of Heav'n did brooding lye,
> And nothing but the Muses Fleece was dry.

Apt too, and anticipating Keats's ' realms
of gold ', is his metaphorical account of his
own absorption in poetry, whereof the spirit

Stolest me away,
And my abused Soul did'st bear
Into thy new-found Worlds, I know not where,
Thy Golden Indies in the Air.

In the *Ode, Sitting and Drinking in the Chair made out of the Reliques of Sir Francis Drake's Ship* we see Cowley's fancy playing freely round a congenial theme, and a poem such as this enables us most easily to answer the question what precisely Cowley's wit was, to understand his explanation of it as containing ' all things '. Wit is the exploitation of a theme, widely and deeply. An episode or an abstract notion is taken and played with, as the Jacobean divine played with a text, illustrating by parallel instances, expounding it in all its possible meanings, linking it up with its cognates, tracing it to its antecedents. Not all the possibilities are ever exhausted in a single poem, but every writer tries to present his theme in a new light and to wring some further drop of meaning out of it. A high degree of fancy and of knowledge is required to play the game successfully. At its best this method really does open new windows for the soul and help the world to grasp a little more of its own meaning. At its worst, as Johnson wrote, ' to write on

12*

their plan it was at least necessary to read
and think. No man could assume the dignity
of a writer by descriptions copied from descriptions, by imitations borrowed from
imitations, by traditional imagery and hereditary similes, by readiness of rhyme, and
volubility of syllables.'

§ 7.

The *Discourses by Way of Essays* give us
Cowley still in early middle age but in retire-
ment, and, we may believe, genuinely contented with it. He is no longer writing for a court
public, but for himself and his friends : and
though he retains, in a greater or less degree,
the poetic habits that he had formed, there
is a return to that simpler, easier way of
writing, as of living, which Cowley suggests
was in accordance with his natural bent. The
prose portions of this collection are perhaps
in higher favour today than the verse, but
they both have the same virtue. They read
like the unforced utterances of a full mind.
To do justice to Cowley's comely and decorous undress you should forget Dryden and
the Queen Anne men and contrast it with the
elaborate full dress or else untidy attire of
his predecessors or contemporaries. His

sentences are of fair length, but we never lose our way in the middle of them ; he never gets out of breath ; he never rants ; he never assumes the judicial solemnity of Bacon. He has colour, variety of rhythm, and the accurate vocabulary which lends distinction to all the earlier English prose before our metaphors were dead and scholarship looked on as pedantry. If we add that what he says is as sensible as his way of saying it, we have fully justified the popularity of his prose essays.

The verses are largely translations: passages, mere snatches some of them, which made a personal appeal to the poet, from Horace, Martial, Virgil, Claudian—the last named represented by an admirable version of the famous lines on the Old Man of Verona. The original pieces are of the same easy, casual nature—interpolations from himself, an English version of his own Latin, improvisations, in only a few cases a full length poem. The eighteenth-century critics were wont to blame Cowley for not writing smoothly, and his prosody has a freedom (it is not necessarily carelessness, for he had well-considered views on the subject) of which even Dryden disapproved and Pope and John-

son emphatically damned. But Cowley could
be musical when he wished, and even in these
familiar verses he can write as elegantly as
any poet need :

> Ah slothful Love, could'st thou with Patience see
> Fortune usurp that flow'ry Spring from thee;
> And nip thy rosie Season with a Cold,
> That comes too soon, when Life's short year grows
>   old.

or,

> Was it for this, that Rome's best blood he spilt
>   With so much falsehood, so much Guilt?
> Was it for this that his ambition strove,
> To equal Caesar first, and after Jove?

or,

> Sleep is a God too proud to wait in Palaces
> And yet so humble too, as not to scorn
>   The Meanest Country Cottages ;
>   His Poppy grows among the Corn.
> The Halcyon Sleep will never build his Nest
>   In any stormy Breast.

or,

> So gracious God, (if it may lawful be
> Among those foolish Gods to mention thee)
> So let me act, on such a private Stage
> The last dull Scenes of my declining Age ;
> After long Toils and Voyages in vain,
> This quiet Port let my toss'd Vessel gain ;
> Of Heav'nly Rest, this Earnest to me lend,
> Let my Life sleep, and learn to love her End.

He never lost the art or the philosophy
which enabled him as a boy to write thus:

> Thus would I double my Life's fading space,
> For he that runs it well, runs twice his Race.

And in this true Delight,
These unbought Sports, this happy State,
I would not fear, nor wish my Fate,
But boldly say each Night,
Tomorrow let my Sun his Beams display
Or in Clouds hide them; I have liv'd to Day.

Clouds may have obscured the brightness
of Cowley's fame. But he was a poet.

SIR JOHN VANBRUGH.

§ 1.

THE acknowledged masters of English comedy may be reckoned on the fingers of one hand—Shakespeare, Jonson, Dryden, Congreve and Sheridan. If the fingers of the second hand are to be used, Vanbrugh must be one of those enumerated, together perhaps with his two contemporaries, Wycherley and Farquhar, with Goldsmith, who as the author of but a single play may hardly claim the highest rank, and with Wilde. Of living authors, following the wisest precedents, I take no count. Future critics may prefer another Irishman for inclusion in this list, but it should not, I think, be to the exclusion of Vanbrugh.

Macaulay, whose review of Leigh Hunt's edition of Vanbrugh and his three great contemporaries is the commonest source of popular knowledge on the subject, did Vanbrugh some disservice. Taking the four writ-

ers in chronological order, he devoted, with
admirable result, so much space to the first
two that he had none left for any detailed
criticism of the second pair, an omission the
more to be regretted in that Vanbrugh was
a lively and entertaining person, of varied
activities and intimately associated with
several of the most picturesque personages
of his age, admirable subject for Macaulay's
portraiture.

It is to be wondered at that no one should
ever have written a life of any length, or even
a monograph, of so famous a man, second only
to Congreve among the playwrights of his
age, and second to none as an architect after
Wren's death, Clarencieux King-of-Arms, a
notable figure in society, and distinguished
by the very particular enmity of the great
Duchess Sarah. Moreover, his life still presents several unsolved problems, notably
those of his early incarceration in the
Bastille and of his apparently protracted
wooing. He was, too, a most frank and lively
letter-writer.

§ 2.

The baptism of John, second son of Giles
Vanbrugh and of Elizabeth his wife, is re-

corded in the register of St. Nicholas Acons,
London, under the date January 24, 1663/4.
The baptisms of an elder brother and of three
sisters are also here recorded. Shortly after
John's birth (having apparently added
another daughter to his family) his father
migrated to Weaver Street, Chester, and the
register of Holy Trinity Church there, from
1667 to 1681, shows the births of seven more
brothers and six more sisters. Of this large
brood thirteen are mentioned in their father's
will, dated 1683. Here John is described as the
eldest son. Giles Vanbrugh was by trade a
sugar baker and a man of good standing. His
father, also Giles (or Gilles), had apparently
come to England from Flanders early in the
17th century. According to Sir John's account,
and as a member of the Heralds' College he
should have had some knowledge of this sort
of thing, he came from Ghent to escape
Alva's Papist zeal. On the other side John
was of good English stock, his mother Elizabeth being a daughter of Sir Dudley Carleton,
of Imber Court, Surrey.

Of Vanbrugh's education nothing is known,
but there is no doubt that he spent his
early manhood in the army and he is subsequently spoken of as 'Captain' Vanbrugh.

His military career, however, is not easy
to follow. In January 1685/6 John Vanbrugh
was granted a commission in Lord Hunt-
ingdon's Regiment. In 1686 he left this
regiment. Next we find, in February
1688/9, Ensign John Brook in the list
of the 14th Foot, Colonel Beveridge's Regiment, and we know that the dramatist
thus spelt his name on occasions. In 1692
Luttrell, the diarist, refers to a case, of which
the Court-martial documents (it was held,
curiously enough, at Bruges) are extant, in
which a Captain Vanbrugh, 'of Colonel Tid-
combe's regiment, late commanded by Colonel
Beveridge deceased,' killed the said Colonel
Beveridge. The evidence showed that Beveridge, who often provoked his inferiors, had
been to blame for the quarrel and that Vanbrugh was of a 'peaceable quiet temper'.
Vanbrugh was acquitted. This may have been
a cousin, Dudley Vanbrugh, whose name, so
spelt, also appears in the list of the 14th Foot
in 1688/9, or John may by this time have received promotion. It is certainly odd that the
variant 'Brook' should in the same list be
used for the name of one cousin and not for
the other.

But in December 1695 we find John Brooke gazetted lieutenant in Col. Thomas Farrington's Regiment, and in the following month John Brooke, Esq., is to be Captain in Lord Berkeley's Marine Regiment, an appointment which, elsewhere, Lord Berkeley is found promising to a Mr. Vanbrook who had been at sea with Lord Carmarthen the year before. Finally, in 1698 the name of Captain John Vanbrook appears in the Home Office list of officers on half pay.

We cannot be sure which, if any, of these references are to Sir John. If all of them, then we must infer that though cleared by court-martial he lost his captaincy in the 14th Foot and served as a lieutenant or even as ensign with some unknown regiment in 1694.

It was during this military part of his career that the episode of the Bastille occurred which has never been fully explained. On February 11th, 1691/2, Luttrell records: 'Last letters from France say three English gentlemen Mr. Vanbrook, Mr. Goddard, and Mr. North were clapt up in the Bastille, suspected to be spyes.' On March 15th he refers to this again : 'French merchants were the other day sent to the Tower to be used as Mr. North and Mr. Vanbroke are

in the Bastille.' There is further, preserved
in the British Museum, ' The humble Petition
of Sir Dudley North ', that one Bertelier, now
in Newgate, be exchanged not for Van Brook
alone, as intended, but for him and Sir
Dudley's brother Montagu North, then in
Toulon Castle.

To this event Vanbrugh himself referred
in a letter of October, 1725, to Tonson in
which he writes that the Duchess of Marlborough 'would like to throw me into an
English Bastille to finish my days as I began
them in a French one'. From this Disraeli
and others have conjectured that Vanbrugh
was born in the Bastille, but by the beginning
of his days Vanbrugh clearly means only the
beginning of his career; just as elsewhere he
writes of marriage that it is ' fitter to end
one's life with than begin it '.

Voltaire *(Letters in England,* XIX, On
Comedy) refers to this episode thus :

> Sir John having taken a tour into France before
> the glorious war that broke out in 1701 was thrown
> into the Bastille and detained there for some time,
> without ever being able to discover the motive which
> had prompted our ministry to indulge him with this
> mark of their distinction. He wrote a comedy during
> his confinement; and a circumstance which appears
> to me very extraordinary is that we don't meet with
> so much as a single satirical stroke against the
> country in which he had been so injuriously treated.

§ 3.

The comedy here referred to is *The Provoked Wife*, but though this may have been the first written, *The Relapse* was the first produced of his plays. This was acted at Drury Lane on December 26, 1696 and was very successful. Nearly a century later Sheridan rewrote it without improving it under the title of *A Trip to Scarbrough*. From now onwards we hear nothing of Vanbrugh as a soldier, much as a playwright, and a little later, as an architect.

Early in the following year *Aesop*, an adaptation from *Les Fables d' Esope*, by Boursault (1638—1701) appeared at Drury Lane, and to the rival theatre in Lincoln's Inn Fields he gave *The Provoked Wife*. After this rapid unloading of his dramatic goods he remained curiously silent. Perhaps Collier's attack on the stage in general and his own work in particular checked his production. His next undertaking was a version of Beaumont and Fletcher's *The Pilgrim*, to which the great Dryden contributed a prologue. This appeared at Drury Lane in 1700. In 1702 appeared at the same theatre his version of *La Traicion busca y castiga* by Francisco de Rojas y Zorrilla, to which he was probably introduced by Le Sage's translation (1700), *Le Traitre Puni.* It is interesting to note that Dancourt, with whose work Vanbrugh was presently to make London familiar, also produced a version of this play, but not till 1707.

In 1704 we find Vanbrugh managing Lincoln's Inn Theatre and associated with Congreve in the production of an unsuccessful and unacknowledged version of Molière's *Monsieur de Pourceaugnac,* acted under the title of *Squire Trelooby.* Next year he opened the Queen's Theatre, Haymarket, a house of his own designing, and here he produced his own version, improved in the rendering, of Dancourt's *Bourgeoises à la Mode* (1692). This is the play known even to the present generation of playgoers as *The Confederacy,* and with Mrs. Bracegirdle and Mrs. Barry and Booth, as Flippanta, Clarissa and Dick Amlet, its success was immediate. Another of Dancourt's plays, *The Country House (La Maison de Campagne),* was produced in the same year at Lincoln's Inn Fields, and a version of Molière's *Le Dépit,* entitled *The Mistake,* later at the Haymarket. But the Haymarket theatre proved a failure, its acoustics being bad, and Vanbrugh retired from the management, apparently without serious loss of money. He had given £ 2000 for the site, so he wrote to Tonson in 1703, ' but have laid out such a scheme of matter that I shall be reimbursed every penny of it by the spare ground '.

His only remaining dramatic piece was the unfinished *A Journey to London,* which Colley Cibber, to whose *Love's Last Shift* his own first play, *The Relapse,* had been a sequel, completed, after its author's death, and produced with great success as *The Provok'd Husband.*

§ 4.

Vanbrugh's career as a playwright overlaps his career as a soldier. His career as an architect overlaps his career as a playwright, but where he served his apprenticeship to that trade it is hard to imagine. The first reference to Vanbrugh in connection with architecture is his appointment as Controller of the Royal Works in 1702, a post to which he was reappointed in 1714, but he can hardly have received this appointment, even in those palmy days of political patronage, without some experience of the duties involved, and in 1703 he mentions that 200 men

13

are working on Castle Howard, one of his greatest undertakings. At the same time he was risking his own and his friends' money on his Haymarket playhouse, and he failed here not in his general architectural skill, but in his treatment of the particular problem of stage acoustics.

He became almost at once the most popular architect of the day. He built Whitton Hall for Sir Godfrey Kneller, who should have been something of a judge. He built Blenheim Palace, a terrible source of worry owing to the parsimonious temper of the Duchess Sarah. He built Old Claremont House, Esher, the Old Clarendon Buildings, Oxford, Greenwich Hospital, half a dozen great country houses, the elephantine church of St. John's, Westminster (a curious structure, not unjustly censured by Leigh Hunt), and several town and suburban houses for himself; one, the Bastille, at Blackheath, evidently named in remembrance of that early imprisonment to which reference has been made. He was knighted in 1714.

Vanbrugh's art has had less than justice done to it by the fame of the epigram (or at least the latter half of it) ascribed to one Abel Evans:

Lie heavy on him earth, for he
Laid many a heavy load on thee.

If Van's buildings were, unlike his plays, heavy and ornate, they were usually imposing and the wits who remarked what splendid ruins they would make,* were paying them the compliment of comparing them, perhaps unconsciously, with the great relics of classical antiquity. They were also, what his plays again in great part were not, original in design.

As a playwright Vanbrugh was a great wit and master of dramatic dialogue, applying his skilful technique to another man's outline. As an Architect he was a bold and wide-visioned artist building boldly to the neglect of a good deal of detail of which a more regular training might have supplied the knowledge, with, perhaps a corresponding loss of breadth and originality. Sir Joshua Reynolds praised Vanbrugh very highly, and it has been generally acknowledged by the critics of this art that in imagination and power of composition he ranks among the great archi-

---

* 'T is Vanbrug's structures that my fancy strike:
Such noble ruins every pile would make,
I wish they'd tumble for the prospect's sake.
The Man of Taste (by the Rev. Mr. Bramston).
Dodsley's Miscellany, I. p. 290.

13*

tects of his nation. He had moreover one quality which many have lacked, reverence for the product of earlier ages. He regretted the destruction of the 200 year old gate of Whitehall and suggested an alternative carriageway through 'the Privy Garden', and on another occasion he deplored the Duke of Rutland's 'improvement' to his house.

§ 5.

Van was a prominent and well-liked personage in the London of his day, and less of a politician than most of his fellow men of letters. He was, in particular, intimate with Congreve, Walsh, Steele, and Nicholas Rowe, the poet laureate, whose *Reconcilement between Jacob Tonson and Mr. Congreve* makes the publisher speak thus of his talented friend :

I'm in with Captain Vanbrugh at the present,
A most sweet-natured gentleman and pleasant.
He writes your Comedies, draws Schemes and Models
And builds Dukes' houses upon very odd hills!
For him, so much I dote on him, that I
(If I were sure to go to heaven!) would die!

. . . .

What if from Van's dear arms I should retire
And warm once more my 'bunnians' at your fire!
If I to Bow Street should invite you home,
And set a bed up in my dining room;
Tell me, dear Mr. Congreve! would you come?

All these were Whigs and, among the politicians, Walpole was a close friend. On the other side, Pope at least treated him civilly and complimented him. Even his satirical lines on Blenheim, which he concludes by declaring ' a house and not a dwelling', give praise where praise is due and are fairer criticism than Pope always cared to express. Swift is said to have disapproved of the morality of Van's plays, which was very absurd of him, for it is no less and the decency rather more than a good many of the lucubrations of himself and his fellow Scribblers can boast.

Both Queen Anne, who paid, while she lived, for the building of Blenheim, and King George, who did not, favoured him, and he had many patrons and friends among the nobility. The Earl of Carlisle, in particular, was both. It was through him that Vanbrugh was appointed Clarencieux King-of-Arms, and should, had not Sir John Anstis got ahead of him, have been Garter. With the Duke of Newcastle he was on sufficiently intimate terms to advise him on his marriage. The bride had the misfortune to be Duchess Sarah's grand-daughter ; but fortunately he could write of her that she,

> I do not think has one grain of this wicked wo-
> man's temper in her : if I did I would not advise
> you to take her tho' with the alloy of a million.

Newcastle shares with Tonson the position
of Vanbrugh's chief correspondent. A little
later (January, 1718/19) he writes to Newcastle announcing his own marriage and refers in characteristic manner to Tonson, who
was one of those amiable people on whom his
friends delighted to inflict gentle chaff:

> Jacob will be frightened out of his wits and his
> religion too when he hears I'm gone at last. If
> he's still in France he'll certainly give himself to
> God, for fear he shou'd now be ravish'd by a
> gentlewoman. I was the last man left between him
> and ruin.

This was evidently a standing jest regarding Tonson. Six months later he adds a post-
script to a letter to Newcastle:

> I have just now an account that a gentleman
> newly arrived from Paris actually saw friend Jacob
> in a frock.

In his next letter he contradicts this
rumour, adding that Jacob, *if he sells now*
stands to make a thousand pounds profit
from his purchase 'in the new company'.
But we have no reason to suppose he did sell
now, any more than Johnny Gay, who lost
the prospect of twice as much in this same
South Sea Bubble.

Vanbrugh had hitherto been a good club-man, a member of the Kit-cat club and also of ' the Tate a Tate club at the Hercules Pillars House in High Holborn ', at which on one occasion ' there was stinking fish and stale cold lamb for supper, with divers liquors made of malt in an execrable manner.' But at last in January 1718/19 he was to marry Mistress Henrietta Maria, eldest child of James Yarburgh, Esquire, Colonel of Foot Guards, of Snaith Hall, Yorks. In connection with this marriage there is another problem not certainly solved, for as early as 1710 we have a description of his courting from the lively pen of Lady Mary Wortley Montague (then Lady Mary Pierrepont), a letter which led Leigh Hunt to date the actual marriage 1710.

> You know (she writes) Van's taste was always odd ; his inclination to ruins has given him a fancy for Mrs. Yarborough: he sighs and ogles so that it would do your heart good to see him.

Lady Mary was then 18, Henrietta Yar-burgh, having been born in 1693, would be 17. Why then ' ruins '? And why the eight years delay in marrying? Mr. Swain, the ' Mermaid ' editor, suggested that Van eventually married a younger sister, but Henrietta is said to have been the eldest child, and in any case one would expect some other reference to this curious development. Either Lady Mary was not referring to the lady's age but merely signifying that she did not approve of her looks, or there is something wrong with the recorded facts. It is hardly possible that it can be Henrietta's mother for whom Van had a *penchant*.*

In August, 1719, their first child was born, ' a bit of a girl popping into the world three months before its time. And the business is all to do over again ', as he wrote to Newcastle.

In spite of his opinion, quoted above, that marriage was best left till late, and in spite of the bad example which so many of his own stage creations had set him, Vanbrugh seems to have had a happy and successful married life. ' I have a good humoured wife,' he writes to Tonson in Paris in November 1719, ' a quiet house and find myself as much disposed to be a friend and servant to a good old acquaintance as ever.' Lady Vanbrugh, he adds, is ready to find Tonson a wife ; ' she has not a sister for you but she knows them that have.' He then says he and his wife will come to dinner, and

* *The Genealogist*, (1878). Vol. 2, pp. 237—40.

Lady Vanbrugh shows that she was at any rate not quite devoid of humour by adding to her husband's letter, 'and if you will make one at cards as I understand you have often done with much finer ladies than I am, I give you my word that I will neither cheat or wrangle. Yr. servt. Hariot V.'

A good many of Vanbrugh's letters of this period are extant, and one of August 8th, 1721, to Newcastle is worth quoting as a specimen of Van's epistolary style :

I was at York all last week. A race every day and a ball every night with as much well look't company as I ever saw got together. The ladys, I mean, in chief. As to the men, the D. of Wharton was the top gallant. The entertainments ending on Friday, he declared, if the company would stay in towne one day more, he wou'd treat the jockeys with a plate, the Ladys with a ball, and all toge-ther with a supper. 'T was done accordingly, and my Lady Milner who had all along been his partner, was now his queen. When supper was ended he invited all the good company to meet him again that day 12 months on the same terms, with many decent and good compliments to the inhabitants of York and Yorkshire for the Honour they did him and hop't 't would do him again. To which they gratefully bowed as who would say, yes. But his grace then bethought him of one civil thing more and said it, "That unless my lady Milner would absolutely engage to be there too he was off, as to the rest of the company." Upon which she look'd she did not know how and all went home to sleep.

Later letters to Tonson contain much entertaining gossip about his own Haymarket projects, the Duke of Newcastle and his guests, the boom in South Sea stock, wherein his brother held £8000, Steele's quarrel with the Lord Chamberlain consequent on his grant of a theatrical license to Wilkes, Cibber and Booth, the Duchess of Marlborough's will, with unmeasured abuse of the Duchess ('D— the Duchess!'), Congreve, gifts of cider from Herefordshire ('Have a care . . . . . some Herefordshire nymph will bounce upon your heart from under an apple tree') and the announcement that he is now 'two boys strong in the nursery'.

This was in June, 1722. Three years later, in August, 1725, Van is again grateful for some 'rare good cider' and describes how, on his way to Castle Howard, he and Lady Vanbrugh passed through Woodstock and were excluded from Blenheim, which their companions visited, by the Duchess's express orders. He goes on :

> You may believe me when I tell you you were often talked of both during the journey and at Stowe and our former Kit-cat days remembered with pleasure. We were one night reckoning who were left behind and both Ld. Carlisle and Ld

Cobham exprest a great desire of having one
meeting next winter if you came to town, not as a
club but old friends that have been a club and the
best club that ever met.

Later in that year he sold his post as
Clarencieux and writes to Tonson again
abusing the Duchess and saying that he
hopes for Walpole's aid against her attempt
to saddle him with the liability for the
building costs of Blenheim.

He died on March 26 of the following
year, 1726, at his house in Scotland Yard
and was buried in St. Stephen's, Walbrook.
His son Charles became ensign in the Cold-
stream Guards and died of wounds received
at Fontenoy. Horace Walpole, writing to
Mann, quotes a letter from Joseph Yorke de-
scribing his death and how he routed a whole
French battalion. Another son is named in
the will of Lady Vanbrugh, who died in 1775.

§ 6.

The fame of the architect has never
equalled that of the man of letters, and even
Macaulay's schoolboy hardly knows the
names of more than three of our great
architects of the past. If Vanbrugh's is one
of them, it is to the fact that he wrote plays
that the distinction is due.

Voltaire, in the essay already quoted, correctly indicates Vanbrugh's crowning, all-sufficing virtue:

> His comedies are more humorous than those of
> Mr. Wycherley but not so ingenious . . . . . Mr.
> Congreve's comedies are the most witty and regular,
> those of Sir John Vanbrugh most gay and humorous.

For the intrigue, or plot, of his pieces he cared little. In point of fact this element is usually provided for him by his French originals. In the case of *The Relapse,* it is in part prescribed by the task he had set himself of providing a sequel to Cibber's play. Only *The Provok'd Wife,* of which the plot is of a common Restoration type, and the unfinished *A Journey to London* are, as far as we know, of wholly independent design.

It is usual to compare Vanbrugh with Congreve, an easy but unfair proceeding, when undertaken by professed admirers of Congreve. For he aimed at none of his friend's intellectual subtlety and brilliant phrasing, while he had qualities of his own which Congreve neither had nor needed. Congreve is a wit, Vanbrugh a humorist. Congreve achieved Meredith's ideal of comedy, a mirthless, intellectual exercise. Vanbrugh's are to these almost farces, cheerful presentations of the foibles of the characters of the time, the city madam and her skin-flint husband, the profligate young rascal of fashion, the new-made peer, the vulgar and loquacious old nurse. Of the two Vanbrugh, for all his foreign extraction and his foreign models, strikes us as the more typically English. His characters are nearer akin to Juliet's nurse, to Falstaff; Congreve's to Volpone, to Tartuffe.

As a translator Vanbrugh is unsurpassed. His dialogue is the most natural and racy that ever was, yet the greater part of it is faithfully taken over from his original. He gives it a liveliness, an ebullience, a dramatic vigour, which make his characters among the most original and vivid on our stage. In this respect *The Confederacy* is the most successful, yet this play is quite a close adaptation of Dancourt. *Les Bourgeoises à la mode* is a good play, *The Confederacy* is a better. Vanbrugh's embellishments, here a little and there a little, emphasize the humour without overstating it, and give colour to Dancourt's neatly sketched but rather monotonous characters. Take at random a speech of Corinna, the enterprising young miss, not yet out of the schoolroom—

a polite version of the inimitable Hoyden in
The Relapse. Here is Dancourt's original:

> *Mariane*—Je ne suis pas à plaindre! Est-il agré-
> able à mon age de vivre éternellement dans la
> solitude? Je n'ai pour toute compagnie que des
> maîtres qui ne m'apprennent que des choses
> inutiles, la musique, la fable, l'histoire, la géo-
> graphie, cela n'est-il pas bien divertissant?
> *Lisette*—Cela vous donne de l'esprit.
> *Mariane*—N'en ai-je pas assez? Ma belle-mère ne
> sait point toutes ces choses, et elle vit heureuse.
> *(Les B. á la M. II, vii.)*

Here is Vanbrugh's rendering:

> *Corinna*—Not pity'd! Why, is it not a miserable
> thing, such a young creature as I am shou'd be
> kept in perpetual solitude, with no other com-
> pany but a parcel of old fumbling masters, to
> teach me geography, arithmetic, philosophy, and
> a thousand things? Fine entertainment, indeed,
> for a young maid at sixteen! methinks one's
> time might be better employed.
> *Flippanta*—These things will improve your wit.
> *Marianna*—Fiddle, faddle; ha'n't I wit enough
> already? My mother-in-law has learn'd none of
> this trumpery, and is not she as happy as the
> day is long?

Vanbrugh has a perpetual flow of high
spirits, yet he never allows himself to ex-
aggerate or to overdo his fun. He keeps his
scenes proportionate to the whole and never
encourages his comedians to settle down to
a knock-about scene regardless of the rest
of the caste, after the fashion of the modern

purveyor of light comedy. His plays abound
in essentially comic situations : Brass black-
mailing his fellow rogue by threatening
merely to talk with an indiscreet loudness ;
the garrison of Sir Tunbelly's house locking
up Miss Hoyden ('let loose' is the delightful term used for the contrary operation)
and getting ready their blunderbuses when
young Fashion comes a-wooing, and a little
later accommodating the true and noble
bridegroom in the dog-kennel; Sir John
Brute, in disguise, brought before the
magistrate; the Headpiece family arriving
in full force in London. Vanbrugh brings out
the comical incongruity of such scenes, but
he never repeats himself and carries his
action on before familiarity has staled the
humour of the situation.

His characters are painted boldly, distinct-
ively and humorously. He is an acute observer, and hits off a likeness in a flash. For
psychological analyses he cares no more
than Corinna would, though like all artists
he has many intuitions of which he is perhaps no better aware than was M. Jourdain
of his prose-speaking faculty.

Unlike Congreve he depicts men better
than women. His Berinthia and Amanda,

Belinda and Araminta are not to be compared with Millamant or Lady Wishfort or An-
gelica. But Lord Foppington, who found
life 'an eternal round O of delight', Brass
and Dick Amlet, even the unpleasant
and sardonic figure of Sir John Brute, and
with them we may set those females of a
different, non-drawing room type, Mrs.
Amlett, and Hoyden and her nurse, these are
characters whose personality comes home to
us so that they remain for ever in the portrait gallery of our memory and so enjoy
immortality among the creatures of fiction.

§ 7.

It is impossible to write of any of the socalled 'Restoration' dramatists without
touching on the vexed question of stage
morality. The society of the age was in
matters of sex singularly lacking in what we
call decency, though it might be more exact
to call it secretiveness or reticence. Anybody
with sufficient wit to write a successful play
must have been sensible of these shortcomings. But the playwright was not a Don
Quixote prepared to assume that things were
what they notoriously were not. The society
depicted was the conventional society of the

age, with, of course, a disproportionate pro-
minence given to the more scandalous aspects
of it. Scenes of domestic bliss were doubtless common enough, but they do not lend
themselves to dramatic treatment and the
cause of morality would not be served by
their presentation. Hardly any dramatist,
certainly not Vanbrugh, expressed any admiration for this state of things; very often
he specifically condemned it. If an immoral
act had a dramatic value he suffered it to
happen. Vanbrugh in the main plot of
The Relapse offended flagrantly, it is
said, in employing a scene of frank seduction.
Do you agree? Do you think on seeing this
scene or reading it that he has offended?
Very well then, he has shown that seduction
is an offensive act. If this sort of thing ex-
cites evil passions, at least it leaves us under
no delusion as to the immorality of the act.
The Puritan logically objected to all stage
love making, because he realised that watch-
ing a man make love on the boards to his
own wife brought the spectator, in his or her
sympathy for the wooer or the wooed,
perilously near to adultery. From any such
insidious provocation to sexual excitement,
at least, such scenes were free. Our conven-

14

tional moral instincts are roused to check
those amorous propensities which beset even
the sturdy Doctor Johnson, when he visited
his friend and pupil's playhouse. But Vanbrugh was not writing ' problem ' plays. The
scene I have referred to is only an incident
in a plot of quite conventional intrigue. Collier was perfectly right in disliking the
contemporary play, but it was not the playwrights who were misleading society but
society which almost inevitably gave unpleasant colour to a stage which, being true
to art and therefore truly related to life, had
to conform in externals to a lax moral code.
The method of the drama is not, as Lamb
protested, realistic, it does not seek to de-
lude the spectator into thinking he is looking
at anything else than a make-believe; but
comedy, however imaginative and intellectual the structure it rears, must rest on a
basis of what men really say and do. In the
next reign the vices of society were more decorously veiled, but the sentimental and
virtuous comedy of Steele lacked the great
essential of comedy—sincerity, or, what
amounts to the same thing, the frank recognition of its own insincerity. Till men
really are good, and not merely trying to be,

a comedy which does not somewhere show the cloven hoof can never wholly please the honest, adult mind.

For Van himself we may fairly ask that he shall be remembered as he was in private life, a gentleman according to the best standards of his day—a loyal and genial friend, an affectionate and dutiful husband, and a man who contributed as much as any man then living to the cheerfulness and comeliness of England. It is with this knowledge of their author's private character that the plays should be read, and it will be seen how purely dramatic are those lines in which, in the words of an old critic, he appears to seek 'to dissuade from chaste love and to recommend by every prurient device the most complete dissoluteness of morals and manners.' Morals which will not withstand the hearing of Heartfree's wooing of Belinda are a poor passport to heaven! This same critic admits that *Æsop* and *The False Friend* 'evince that he possessed right moral feelings and that they were only perverted on sexual topics by the profligacy of the times.' In truth there is no better ground for convicting Vanbrugh of immorality on the score of actions performed by his characters than

14*

there is for convicting Aeschylus of matri-
cide, or Sophocles of incest, or Shakespeare
of wife-murder.

Vanbrugh resembles Fielding (who much
esteemed his comedy). He knew men's frailties and deplored them, but he did not blink
those faults, neither was he prepared to
damn his five good parts for the sake of his
one even flagrantly bad one. There is much
charity towards men and women in the words
he puts into the mouth of Berinthia (in *The
Relapse)*, a young woman by no means im-
maculate, but not the heroine, that rôle
being filled by the triumphantly virtuous
Amanda:

> Well, there's nothing upon earth astonishes me
> less when I consider what they and we are compos'd
> of. For nature has made them children, and us
> babies.

JOHN GAY.

§ 1.

JOHNNY GAY is not and never has been looked upon as in the first rank of English poets. Nobody coming blithely home carolling snatches from *The Beggar's Opera,* as all London has at some time done under both the first and the fifth George, has thought of what he has just heard as the work of a great poet. Yet Gay has never lacked his readers and his lovers, and his poetic gifts were of such a quality as should make their possessor's art a thing of real and permanent value.

But Gay had in him, along with a rare talent, fatal defects of character, and circumstances unhappily favoured the development of his inferior qualities. Everybody who knew him loved Johnny, and it is hard to speak evil of so amiable a creature, but

Courthope, no prejudiced witness against
any of the Augustans, has described him as
'greedy, indolent and ostentatious'. He
wanted applause, he wanted ease—a warm,
cosy place in the fashionable world. On the
whole he got what he wanted; had it not been
for the South Sea bubble he might have died a
rich man; as it was he never suffered from not
being one, though the frustrated expectation
made him rather querulous. But for this
mess of pottage he sacrificed his birthright,
his kinship with Herrick and with Burns as
a singer of country joys and the natural
beauty of the world :

> No more I'll sing Buxonia brown
> Like goldfinch in her Sunday gown
>
> .   .   .   .   .   .
>
> But Landsdown fresh as flower of May
> And Berkeley lady blithe and gay.

and Anglesey and Hyde and Montague. Thus
he became the third of the trio of poets
among the Brothers, who frequented Ozin-
da's chocolate house in St. James's Street,
instead of singing the songs of his native
Devon*.

---

* Leigh Hunt refers to him as "the good-hearted,
the natural man in the midst of the sophisticate".
In both, perhaps, there was something of the qualities
of a Boythorne.

§ 2.

Gay was born at Barnstaple and baptised there on September 16, 1685, the year of Sedgemoor. He was educated at the local Grammar School, along with William Fortescue, afterwards Master of the Rolls, legal advisor to the Scriblerus Club, and author of that amusing skit Stradlyng v. Stiles, and with Pope's friend Aaron Hill. He was apprenticed to a silk-mercer of London, but is said to have disliked trade and won an early return to Barnstaple. Nevertheless, he must have gone back to London very soon, probably before the publication, in 1708, of his first poem *Wine,* in which he imitates John Phillip's *Cider* (1706). He was now a diligent reader of the great periodical literature of the day, frequenting, we may presume, the coffee-houses for whose *habitués* it was designed. In 1711 he produced a pamphlet discussing the chief newspapers, notably *The Tatler* and *The Spectator* on the one side, and *The Examiner* on the other. He adroitly contrived to win the favour of both the rival editors, Steele and Swift, and a little later of Pope; and this led to his undertaking, to order, his *Shepherd's Week,* a counterblast to Ambrose (Namby-Pampy) Phillips' *Pasto-*

rals. Here Gay's natural genius for 'country
sentiment' was sufficiently subdued to
permit him to please his town-bred audience,
and he was henceforward one of the most
applauded members of the Harley-Boling-
broke-Pope-Swift *coterie,* sharing in their
political spoils and, in no long time, in their
political disgrace.

The earliest notable fruit of this association was *"The What D'Ye Call It",* a Tragi-
Comi-Pastoral Farce, which first won the
plaudits of the town in the early days of
1715. In 1717 he joined Pope and Arbuthnot in
another farce, *Three Hours after Marriage,*
a piece of less merit than might have seemed possible were coalitions less notoriously
unsuccessful. In 1716 appeared his *Trivia,*
wherein he applies to London his great
powers of observation and of description in
verse. Four years later he published a collection in two handsome folio volumes of his
poems, in which were included, in addition
to the pieces mentioned, such other occasional poems as he had from time to time composed. His profits from this publication,
amounting to over £1000, were lost in the
pricking of the South Sea Bubble. There was,
however, more than one Mæcenas in that age

ready to befriend so fashionable a poet, and even the Whigs seem to have had a weakness for Johnny. He held a post as Lottery Commissioner, worth £150 a year, from 1722 to 1731, in spite of his supposed activity as a political satirist.

Meanwhile he wrote another play, *The Captives*, and in 1727 published his *Fables*, dedicated to the young Duke of Cumberland, whose tutor he now was. Then in 1728, after a long incubation, appeared the famous *Beggar's Opera*, which was followed by a far inferior sequel, *Polly*, the publication of which was made immensely profitable by its suppression, for political reasons, on the stage. The Duchess of Queenberry offended ministers by her ardent championship of Gay and his prohibited opera, and was banished from court in consequence. Under her protection, and the Duke's, Gay lived at Amesbury till his death on December 4, 1732. Two days before Christmas he was buried in Westminster Abbey, in Poets' corner.

§ 3.

In the age that immediately succeeded his own Gay was held in repute chiefly as a fabulist. Later, when naturalism became the

fashion, critics extolled Gay as a truthful de-
lineator, in an artificial age, of the scenes
and customs of real England. In both respects Gay's greatness is at best only com-
parative. In the one case he achieved success
in a form where verse competes on no more
than equal terms with prose. In the second
he writes well enough only to tantalize us
that he should not have written more and
better. His few wild-flowers star the trim
verdure of the Popian lawn. They would not
take the eye growing in the woodlands and
meadows of other districts.

But in a third province, where his contemporary fame, though great, was not due so
much to his literary merit as to topical,
social and scandalous considerations, a recent revival, following on a long earlier
stage career, has proved the high, positive
value of Gay's work. *The Beggar's Opera*
owes much to its music, fuller than any
Opera before or since of pure, graceful airs,
springs of melody, sweet and untainted by
false sentiment or affectations of technique.
To our own age this came as a revelation,
and the unmusical and the expert alike joined
in praising and enjoying this rediscovery of

a forgotten mode of art. ' What a joy it was,'
wrote a poet critic.*

> 'What a joy it was to hear English music once
> more! . . . . . the music of the English soil, so noble,
> so gay, so debonair, so beautiful. The music that
> grew in England like wayside flowers, of which
> Purcell wove garlands, which the cavalier soldiers
> put in their velvet hats, and the soldiers of the
> Georges wore as a cockade or flung to the girls they
> left behind them ; flowers which were neglected for
> many years until Sullivan planted his rollicking
> border.'

To these airs Gay wedded words which
never occasion the poetic thrill, but are
always comely and neat. No one with an ear
for this kind of thing can fail to note the
superiority of the phrasing and rhythm of
these lyrics over those of the ordinary opera.
Sung by a singer who has thoughts for something better than the mechanism of his own
voice, it is a pleasure to hear the natural
and tripping sentences of Gay's witty, dainty
muse. If the music suggests to Mr. Baring
the name of Sullivan, the neatness of the
rhymes, never sating with excessive ingenuity, suggests Gilbert. And as in that
famous Victorian partnership, it is the
absolute fitness of this marriage of words
and tune that so notably satisfies the ear and

* Maurice Baring in *"The London Mercury."*

the mind. Anybody who remembers the words will remember the numbers, and *vice versa*. The one inevitably suggests the other. In some cases, of course, the association is traditional; Gay introduces into his own lyric the old refrain—' Over the hills and far away ', for example; in others he achieves as much success with his own material, as in this unpretentious little song :

> Before the barndoor crowing,
> The cock by hens attended,
> His eyes around him throwing,
> Stands for a while suspended.
> Then one he singles from the crew,
> And cheers the happy hen
> With how do you do, and how do you do,
> And how do you do again.

§ 4.

But it is not by reason of its lyrics that the reader will prize *The Beggar's Opera*. It is a comedy, very light, but of most rare and admirable quality. The irony of it is so keen and so excellently sustained that we are not surprised to learn that it was Swift, the master ironist of our literature, who in 1721, first suggested the theme of a Newgate pastoral, and we suspect that he had more than one finger in the piece. Assume the moral premisses of Macheath and Jem Twitcher and the piece proceeds to as logical an unfolding of an edifying plot as any senti-mental romance. The resemblance to Field-ing's *Jonathan Wild* (about 15 years young-er) is obvious and plainly not due to accident. The motives of the play are indicated, better than by any epitome of the plot, by some of the ' characteristics ', quoted from the text of the play, which worthy John Bell set on the title page of his edition:

'T'is but fitting we should protect and encourage cheats, since we live by 'em.

Let Betty Sly know that I'll save her from trans-portation, for I can get more by her staying in England.   *Peachum.*

Any private dispute of mine shall be of no ill consequence to my friends.

I love the sex, and a man who loves money might as well be contented with one guinea as I with one woman.   *Macheath.*

Pox take the tailors for making the fobs so deep and narrow!

I would not willingly forfeit my honour by be-traying any body.   *Filch.*

Why are the laws levelled at us? are we more dishonest than the rest of mankind? What we win, gentlemen, is our own by the law of arms and the right of conquest.   *Jemmy Twitcher.*

Of tried courage and indefatigable industry.
       Robin of Bagshot.

Away, hussy, hang your husband and be dutiful.
       Mr. Peachum.

What, murder the man I love! The blood runs cold at the very thought of it.   *Polly.*

> Had'st thou been hanged five months ago I had
> been happy—for I love thee so that I could sooner
> bear to see thee hanged than in the arms of another.
> *Lucy Lockitt.*

From these sentences the ingenious may deduce the trend of the whole. All the characters are vicious and fit denizens of Newgate. But the professed criminals have wit, courage, and generosity, and observe honour among thieves. The gaoler and those who have evaded the law have no redeeming qualities. But are we shocked at the immoral proceedings which the play sets before our eyes? Not at all, not the most rigid moralist among us. Not a word is spoken in praise of true virtue, and breaches of all the ten commandments are acquiesced in without any apparent demur by this scandalous author. Yet we laugh at the broad humour and clever irony and feel no incongruity in the wedding of this rakish libretto with that gay and innocent music.

How is this? There are, I think, two answers. Most people may be appeased with the first and will not require a second. But some self-tormenting souls will.

The first is the old defence put forward by Charles Lamb on behalf of Restoration comedy—the absence of any sense of illusion ; and it is a far better defence in Gay's case, for his comedy presents a society quite unlike any that any audience that mattered could possibly feel at home in, so as to find in its behaviour examples, good or bad, for its own conduct. The cynical immorality of Wycherley's or Congreve's beaux and belles might mislead : no one could possibly be instigated to petty larceny by Filch or to polygamy by Macheath. We admire the gallant, swaggering Macheath, pretty, amorous Polly, and Macheath's tattered and roistering band. We do not think of their moral standards, these are reprehensibly low, but they are taken for granted—forgotten, so long as they are constant, as these, with no truly virtuous characters in the play, are. The thing is frankly artifice, and the alleged author is brought on the stage at either end to make sure we shall not forget it. 'In this kind of drama', remarks the Beggar, in an apology for the happy ending, 'by request', 'tis no matter how absurdly things are brought about '.

But for those who positively refuse to allow themselves to consider anything divorced from its moral bearings, there is a further consideration. In all art the range

of light and shade is never so wide as in
nature. It suffices if the gradations are kept
apparently to scale. This, within Rembrandt-
esque limits, Gay achieves. All his characters are decidedly subfusc, for even our dear
Polly has not, we fear, been greatly careful
of her virtue when her heart has been touched, and is not above living on the fruits of
her highwayman husband's industry. But
from Polly downwards the characters sink to
such Stygian depths of blackness that the
virtues of the ' good ' shine with a beautiful
lustre, smutched and spotted though they
really be. Moreover, Gay is careful, in the
person of his Beggar, to remind us that the
whole thing may fittingly be transposed to a
higher key :

> 'Through the whole Piece you may observe such
> a similitude of manners in high and low life that
> it is difficult to determine whether (in the fashion-
> able vices) the fine gentlemen imitate the gentlemen
> of the road, or the gentlemen of the road the fine
> gentlemen. Had the Play remained as I at first
> intended, it would have carried a most excellent
> moral ; 't would have shewn that the lower sort of
> people have their vices in a degree as well as the
> rich, and that they are punished for them.'

The austere moralist may claim that all
human character is so immeasurably short
of perfection that whether we place our hero

a few rungs higher or lower on the ladder of moral progress matters not, so long as the relative degrees are observed. Absolutely we may not call any man good. By comparison, Macbeath and Peachum are as Orlando and Ganelon.

§ 5.

It was the political allegory which, with very little reason that the modern eye can detect, was read into the play that made its production so great a social success. A few hits at lawyers and politicians there are, but no one reading the play today, still less seeing it played, would associate Macheath with the Prime Minister. The truth is that literature under the patronage system was so inevitably connected with politics that for a Tory poet or playwright to score a success was in itself a blow to the Whigs, even though the success might be achieved by something as remote from politics as a pastoral poem, a translation of Homer, or an edition of Shakespeare. Swift and his fellows of the Scriblerus Club were marked men. Just as a professed wit, it is said, has only to ask for the salt to raise a roar of laughter, so these

15

writers had only to produce a play to set
the politicians talking.*

In the case of *Polly* this procedure was
carried to the height of absurdity. *Polly* is a
sequel to *The Beggar's Opera* and sadly inferior to that brilliant piece. Macheath,
transported to Virginia, turns pirate and
heads a war against the planters and the
Indians. For love of Jenny Diver, his be-
trayer in the original play, and to evade his
other loves, he disappears as Macheath and
reappears as Morano, a coloured gentleman
and a born pirate-king. To them enter Polly,
heiress of the lately hanged Peachum, in
search of her husband. However, true virtue,
in the untutor'd mind of a poor Indian, Cawwaukee, now appears, and in the end
Macheath is killed and Polly wedded, *en sec-
ondes noces,* to this gallant prince. Again
there are a few passing references to political corruption and a certain amount of satire
at the expense of the militia. But the ministry, remembering the success of *The
Beggar's Opera,* was afraid of what the
critics of the coffee-houses and drawing-

---

* Addison's *Cato*, it will be remembered, had been
used as the occasion for a demonstration by both
parties, each interpreting it according to its own
principles.

rooms might make of it. In itself it might
appear harmless enough, but who could foresee what the perverse ingenuity of the Tory
wits might not read into it—and aloud. So
they forbade the stage performance of the
piece ; and thereby made the fortune of the
printed book and of its author.

This fortune went lightly and was lightly
won. *Polly* is not worthy of the adorable
Miss Peachum's name. The introduction of
true virtue in the person of Cawwaukee,
stage figure though he is, disturbs the scale
of moral values. Macheath becomes a tawdry
and sordid ruffian, Polly a sentimental young
person. The gibes at the rich, instead of
being implied in the allegory, are expressed in the portrayal of Mr. Ducat. So lament-
able is the falling off, particularly in the
irony, that it is hard not to suspect that
there is to all intents and purposes a change
of authorship, that Gay is now the sole cook,
whereas before the dish had owed its flavour
to that *cordon blue,* the Dean of St. Patrick's,
now (1728) in Ireland.

§ 6.

Gay's third opera is pretty generally
ignored, but it is (leaving the music out of

15*

the question) not only a much better piece
than Polly, but possesses features of particular interest. *Achilles* is a kind of heroic
comedy, of a type for which Gay in the
Prologue claims the merit of novelty. The
claim is just. There is not, I think, any play
of this kind which Gay is likely to have
known, though the comic treatment of heroic
figures is characteristic of the earlier English drama and there are obvious points of
resemblance to Lyly's court comedy.

The scene is the court of Lycomedes, king
of Scyros, where Achilles, under the name of
Pyrrha and in the guise of a maiden, has
been placed by his mother, Thetis, to save
him from the doom that awaits him on the
plains of Ilium. Lycomedes is enamoured of
the supposed Pyrrha and woos her first by
proxy and then in person. Achilles checks
their advance with Homeric vigour. Meanwhile Queen Theaspe, not unreasonably
jealous of her husband, has set her daughter,
Deidamia, in closest intimacy with Pyrrha
so as to make sure the amorous king shall
have no chance of access to his fair guest.
She also plans to marry Pyrrha to her
nephew Periphas, who has no wish to marry,
and thereby involves him in a quarrel with

that mighty man of valour Ajax, who has
come to collect the Scyrian levies and has
also fallen a victim to the beauty of the hope
of Hellas. Finally, in faithful accordance
with the old legend, Ulysses and Diomede
arrive, disguised as merchants, and by ex-
posing, amid the bales of women's fairings, a
soldier's habiliments makes 'that careless
creature Pyrrha who hath not once thought
of her clothes' bewray herself. Achilles, torn
between Ares and Aphrodite, weds Deidamia,
and then follows the drums and trumpets to
the field. Ulysses, who has the last word,
withdraws to the tune of a 'Saraband of
Corelli'.

This is an amusing plot, handled with
admirable propriety, and the dialogue is
easy and witty. It is a slight piece, playing
only on the surface with the foibles of humanity and the humours of artificial situations. But of its kind it is good and coming
from an age which produced hardly a comedy
worthy of the name, after Farquhar and
before Colman, it deserves higher praise
than it has received. It succeeded on the
stage at its first appearance and may be
read today with a good deal of pleasure.

§ 7.

A brief tribute is also due to one of Gay's earlier dramatic pieces, which, though not an opera, might to a discerning eye have marked Gay down as a skilful writer of light libretto. This is *The What D'Ye Call It,* a trifling confection, a mere matter of some hour's traffic of the stage, but one that needed a light hand. It is a proof of the genuine wit of the piece that such a production, a skit on the dramatic modes of the day, should have retained its stage popularity even beyond its models' vogue, and should even today be a most readable little play. The plot is quite absurd, but not more than befits burlesque; the dialogue is lively and pointed, and the only lyric, with its neatly handled feminine (or dissyllabic) rhymes, is one of the most tuneful set of verses of the age :—

> The merchant, rob'd of pleasure,
> Sees tempests in despair;
> But what's the loss of treasure
> To losing of my dear?
> Should you some coast be laid on
> Where gold and di'monds grow,
> You'd find a richer maiden,
> But none that loves you so.

We may believe that Gay's was the main hand in the elaboration of this piece, albeit

Cibber appears disposed to give Pope that
credit. Certainly in this song sounds the
authentic note of *The Beggar's Opera,* and
the cheerful irresponsibility of the whole is
such as we especially associate with Gay.
Steele is said to have seen in the play, to his
indignation, an irreverend mockery of Addison's solemn tragedy of *Cato;* others, after
the fashion of the age, professed to discern
in it a satire on the late war. These things
are a measure of the author's (or authors')
success in provoking the interest of the
town ; they afford no indication of the real
temper of the piece.

§ 8.

Gay's non-dramatic work has received
more attention and needs less. Its qualities,
good and bad, are evident. He could write
smoothly and aptly about pretty nearly anything. But he never achieved the pithiness
or the grace of Mat. Prior, or the brilliant,
though sometimes immodest, wit and realism
of Swift. As for Pope, Gay's verse seems
thin and crude beside the rich and mellow
honey of his utterance. A knowledge of
nature Gay certainly had, but it may be
doubted if he had much feeling for it. He was

ashamed of the scent of hay that now and
then entered the chambers of his poetry, and
would apologize for it, proceeding to speak
slightingly of 'dung-heaps.' His rural knowledge served to expose the artificialities of
his rival, but he does not for all that allow it
to be his own inspiration. His country Muse
sings to him her artless and beautiful melo-
dies, and he does but use her to amuse his
fine, scornful friends of the Town, himself
joining in their mockery.

Rural Sports, in which Gay shows a very
accurate knowledge of his subject (particularly of angling), is by far the best of his
country pieces. But he writes very neatly,
and his verses amuse by a kind of quaint
solemnity:

Ah, Bouzybee, why did'st thou stay so long?
The mugs were large, the drink was wondrous strong!
Thou should'st have left the fair before 't was light,
But thou sat'st toping till the morning light.

It is this, together with a remarkably keen
eye for the humours of London streets,
that makes his *Trivia* a poem of real distinction. There is no poem in the language of
quite this type. There are no scenes in it so
vivid as Swift's *City Shower,* but even in
prose so droll and so truthful a description
of the sights and ways of London would be

worth having. Gay's pleasant, quizzical, easy-paced verse makes it more memorable and more pointed.

> Experienced men, inured to city ways,
> Need not the Calendar to count their days.
> When through the town with slow and solemn air,
> Led by the nostril, walks the muzzled bear;
> Behind him moves majestically dull,
> The pride of Hockley-hole, the surly bull;
> Learn hence the periods of the week to name;
> Mondays and Thursdays are the days of game.

How wise, to this day, is such advice as this, and how simply yet distinctly phrased :

> When waggish boys the stunted besom ply
> To rid the shabby pavement: pass not by
> Ere thou hast held their hands; some heedless flirt
> Will over-spread thy calves with spattering dirt.
> Where porters hogsheads roll from carts aslope,
> Or brewers down steep cellars stretch the rope,
> Where counted billets are by carmen toss'd,
> Stay thy rash step, and walk without the post.

In the *Fables,* Gay's command of easy versification is fully displayed and his moral is plain and salutary. More than this cannot be said for these once famous pieces. They lack both the racy wit of the folk-lore fable, and the shrewd humour of Chaucer's brilliant study of galline psychology, the Nonne Preste's Tale of Chanticleer and Pertelote. Gay's animals are conventional and the stories decidedly dull. He is out to edify, and his lively verse and neat phrasing can-

not give his apologues that pith and point
which the mode requires. In the second book
the satire is almost wholly political and not
at all impressive. Too often instead of getting
to work on his story Gay begins with a moral
harangue in such pedantic strain as this :

> We frequently misplace esteem
> By judging men by what they seem.
> To birth, wealth, power, we should allow
> Precedence and our lowest bow:
> In that is due distinction shown:
> Esteem is virtue's right alone.

The mild zeugma in the fourth line is the
only glimmer of wittiness in style here, and
such passages remind us only too forcibly
of later examples of the species to which,
after all, these *Fables* of Gay's belong by
origin, the moral poem for children.

Finally, let us praise that charming ballad,
doubly welcome from an age when ballads
were infrequent, *Sweet William's Lament
to Black-eyed Susan*. Nothing else of Gay's
belongs to this class or possesses quite this
quality. It is full of melody, which is nothing
to surprise us coming from the author of *The
Beggar's Opera* lyrics, and full of vivid
picturings :

> William, who high upon the yard
>   Rocked with the billow to and fro,
> Soon as her well-known voice he heard

> He sigh'd and cast his eyes below:
> The cord slides swiftly through his glowing
> > [hands]
>
> And (quick as lightning) on the deck he stands.

Very simple and very dramatic. Beautiful is the simile in the third stanza :

> So the sweet lark, high pois'd in air,
> > Shuts close his pinions to his breast
> (If, chance, his mate's shrill call he hears)
> > And drops at once into her nest.
> The noblest captain in the British fleet
> Might envy William's lips those kisses sweet.

All eight stanzas have charm, and it is to be regretted that Gay did not write more of this sort. Perhaps, had he lived his life out in Barnstaple, he might. Perhaps, on the other hand, he would never have taken to versifying at all. *The Beggar's Opera,* too, in spite of Swift, would probably never have been written ; certainly not by Gay.

GEORGE MACDONALD.

§ 1.

IT IS perhaps natural that in the course of that inevitable reaction by which the world seems to progress we should depreciate the value of our fathers' and grandfathers' art. Fashions in literature seem to recur in cycles of little less than three centuries, and it may be well on in the twenty-second century that Victorianism will come into its own again. Today, certainly, the writers of that age are already more or less in eclipse, and the novel, which as the youngest of our literary forms moves most quickly, shows this phenomenon most clearly of all. Even Dickens and Thackeray totter on their thrones ; Bulwer Lytton is as dead as the Czar ; George Eliot, Trollope, Charles Reade and the rest accumulate dust on the shelves of our ' gentlemen's libraries '.

With them has passed George MacDonald, a writer never among the very greatest in

repute among his own generation, but one
who had certain merits in as high a degree
as any one in our literary history. He was
definitely and avowedly a Christian teacher;
strongly, even bitterly (as far as the word
may be used of a good man) undenomina-
tional, and tending always to a mysticism
with which his age was in small sympathy,
but never getting away from the standpoint
of practical Christian ethics.

Unfortunately for MacDonald's popularity
most readers of 'religious' fiction are secta-
rian, while those average people who
'profess and call themselves Christian' and
are content with that, are averse from anything that is demonstratively pious. The
critically instructed cry, 'A novel with a
purpose!'—and turn to a novel of which the
purpose is merely commercial. MacDonald is
an artist and his aim is to create a beautiful
image which may inspire the world to make
itself more beautiful. But human character,
which is what MacDonald represents, is then
in his eyes most beautiful when it is most
Christlike, so that his heroes have always in
them, as far as human frailties permit, something of the spirit of Christ. Of theology
there is none in his novels, of doctrine there

is much, but it is never more than the dramatic situation permits, a true expression of a
character whose actions are intimately connected with the plot; and the value of his
morality lies in this fact, that he depicts
Christian virtue not in the abstract or
cloistered but in action and on the battle-
field of his own countyside.

§ 2.

George MacDonald was born at Huntly in
Aberdeenshire in the year 1824. He was a
Celt, and his native mysticism was in no
way driven out of him by his upbringing in
the strict Calvinist doctrine. Of his school-
days at the local school and his college days
in Aberdeen his many fictional representa-
tions of these things give, cumulatively, a
full and faithful picture. We cannot be
mistaken in figuring him as suffering under
the tawse of a well-meaning but mechanically minded dominie; being drilled into a
knowledge of the vernacular and classical
languages; admiring the alien culture of
some southron lady; spending happy holidays
out on the farm; going by coach or by foot,
to the granite city to sit for a bursary; then
passing through the various stages from

bejan to *magistrand*. At this point the seek-
er after autobiography might well be misled
into thinking that medicine rather than the
Kirk was his hero's destination, for Christ
and the Christlike man, in MacDonald's most
usual presentation, are healers of mankind,
not priests. It was, however, for the ministry
that MacDonald was intended and he was
actually licensed to a church at Arundel in
Sussex, after a course of study at a theological college in north London.

But theology, distinct from practical morality, had for him no interest, and his flock,
who battened only on the food they were
used to, complained of his lack of sound
doctrinal learning. Whereupon MacDonald
gave up the ministry and became a free-
lance, serving Christ as best he might,
preaching without payment in any pulpit
and eventually joining the Church of England, but as a layman and reserving his right
to preach to congregations of any denomin-
ation. He settled in Hammersmith, living in
the house which came later to be known as
Kelmscott House. He had a wide acquaintance
among the intellectuals of the day, and his
personality enforced the sane, virile, moral
influence of his writing. He wrote novels,

mystic and historical romances, literary and
religious essays, and poetry, and in everything, if he did not attain equal success, he
expressed alike his own strong and sincere
character, which enabled him to appeal to
every degree and to every age.

The list of his books is a long one and it is
hard to resist the impression that he wrote
with too great facility. It is not that he ever
wrote anything that was not worth writing
or that did not come from his heart, but he did
not always avoid a tendency to follow too
readily the line of least resistance, which
leads here to a slightly conventional turn in
his plot, there to the repetition of a minor
trait or incident in one of his other books.
Yet even as I hint a fault I feel it would not
be easy wholly to substantiate it. Most of the
stuff of MacDonald's novels is taken from
the life, and his characters have interests
and experiences closely akin to his own.
Snowball fights; great floods; medical studies; instrumental music; a rather curious
regard for India as a home of mystic philosophy and great wealth; a fondness for dumb
animals, particularly dogs and horses;
'unco guid' ministers and other ministers
not so good but even more given to 'bleth-

er '; religiously-minded working men, shep-
herds, usually, or soutars ; repentant Magda-
lens ; little girls, precocious and abnor-
mally sensitive to the latent spiritual qualities in their robust boy companions ; vicious
young lairds; young women of a more cultured English type, markedly Victorian ; these,
and a little too much in the ' airy, fairy
Lilian ' manner—the reader of any two or
three of MacDonald's novels will recognize
almost all these ingredients. Yet it is unfair
to suggest that they ever become stale with
use. They are the fit material of a story
which comes from the author's imagination
and heart, as well as from his brain and his
experience. A great many of the novels in-
troduce the same characters, and MacDonald,
though he lived his later years in England,
wrote best when his scenes and personages
were those which had impressed his imaginative boyhood.

§ 3.

Robert Falconer is by general consent the
first among the novels. Robert himself takes
rank as one of the great creations of literature, and it is, when all is done, by the
vividness and originality of their characters

that novels take a permanent place among
the classics. He has all the qualities which
MacDonald would have us most reverence,
utter sincerity, notably in rejecting the
harsh austerities of his grandmother's Cal-
vinism, and a noble piety which expresses
itself in a desire to serve, to live up to the
spirit of Christ's great injunction 'thou
shalt love thy neighbour as thyself'. Robert's childhood is painted with extraordinary skill. With his faithful henchman Shar-
gar, his intemperate friend 'Dooble Sanny',
and his well-loved fiddle, we know him and
his way of living and thinking as fiction
seldom helps us to know its personages;
and to know these folk, thorough rascals
though one of them was in the world's eyes,
is to love them. 'Dooble Sanny' is again
typical of MacDonald's favourites. He has
many vices, but he could love much and to
him much is forgiven. Always we feel that
MacDonald's sympathies are with Fielding
rather than with Richardson, and though
Tom Jones was far too licentious a young
man to make a suitable hero for one of Mac-
Donald's books, in his freedom from hypocrisy he possesses the one indispensable
(though by no means all-sufficing) virtue.

16*

The Calvinistic old Mrs. Falconer, in whose
heart humanity is ever struggling with a
narrow, dogmatic religion, is as fine a
character study, on a smaller scale, as her
grandson, and it is the home scenes in which
all these admirable characters figure that
make the real greatness of the novel. The
whole Kail-yard school never bettered this
as a presentation of village life.

There are many moving passages and situations in the story. I will mention only
two. Robert's father had deserted his family
before the story opens, and his wife is now
dead. His mother, though she fronts the
world proudly and austerely, spends her
life in secret prayer that her son may yet be
convinced of sin and repent and be saved
before he dies. When at last she gets
seemingly certain news of his death but none
of the prayed for repentance, she is stricken
to the heart, and at the same time more deter-
mined than ever that no weakness on her
part shall make easy the path of destruction
for her grandson. Meanwhile, Robert, at the
bidding of his heart, has rejected his grandmother's pessimistic acceptance of doom. His
eventual resolve is to find and redeem his
father, whom he will not believe dead; but

long ere that is arrived at he has dared to
rebel, and his rebellion comforts his grandmother against all her convictions. The
passage in which the pious rebel expresses
his faith in God's mercy is a fine one, written,
like all MacDonald's most moving utterances, in Scots. After Sunday supper and the
Bible reading, Robert turns the conversation to the subject of Christ's suffering for
the sins of the world. From this he proceeds
to proclaim his solution of the problem of
his father's damnation :

> 'A' them 'at sits doon to the supper o' the Lamb
> 'll sit there because Christ suffert the punishment
> due to their sins—winna they, grannie?'
> 'Doobtless, laddie.'
> 'But it'll be some sair upo' them to sit there
> aitin' an' drinkin' an' talkin' awa', and enjoyin'
> themsel's, whan ilka noo an' than there'll come a
> sough o' wailin' up frae the ill place, an' a smell o'
> burnin' ill to bide.'
>
> .   .   .   .
>
> 'Duv ye think, grannie, that a body wad be
> allowed to speak a word i' public, like, there—at the
> long table, like, I mean?'
> 'What for no, gin it was dune wi' modesty, and
> for a guid rizzon? But railly, laddie, I doobt ye're
> haverin' a' thegither. Ye hard naething like that,
> I'm sure, the day, frae Mr. Maccleary.'
> 'Na, na; he said naething aboot it. But maybe
> I'll gang and speir at him, though.'
> 'What aboot?'

'What I'm gaein' to tell ye, grannie.
'Well, tell awa', and hae dune wi't.'

.   .   .   .

'Well, gin I win in there, the verra first nicht
I sit down wi' the lave o' them, I'm gaein' to rise
up and say—that is gin the Maister, at the head o'
the table, disna bid me sit doon—an' say: "Brithers
an' sisters, the haill o' ye, hearken to me for ae
minute; an' O Lord! gin I say wrang jist tak the
speech frae me, and I'll sit doon dumb an' rebukit.
We're a' here by grace and no by merit, save His,
as ye a' ken better nor I can tell ye, for ye hae
been langer here nor me. But it's jist ruggin' and
rivin' at my hert to think o' them 'at's doon there.
Maybe ye can hear them. I canna. Noo, we hae nae
merit, an' they hae nae merit, an' what for are we
here and them there? But we're washed clean and innocent noo; and noo, whan there's nowyte lying upo'
oursel's it seems to me that we micht beir some
o' the sins o' them 'at hae ower mony. I call upo'
ilk ane o' ye 'at has a frien or a neebor down yonner,
to rise up an' taste nor bite nor sup mair till we
gang up a' thegither to the fut o' the throne, and pray
the Lord to lat's gang and du as the Maister did
afore's, and bier their griefs, and cairry their
sorrows down in hell there: gin it may be that they
may repent and get remission o' their sins, an' come
up here, wi' us at the lang last, and sit doon wi's at
this table, a' throuw the merits o' oor Saviour
Jesus Christ, at the heid o' the table there. Amen."

This naive refusal of the doctrine of
eternal damnation is characteristic of Mac-
Donald, but it comes with wonderful dramatic force in its context. This simple and
logical application of the root principles of

Christianity supplies a motive in almost all MacDonald's other novels.

Another fine and finely used incident is Mrs. Falconer's sacrificial burning, in an excess of puritanic zeal, of Robert's beloved and valuable fiddle, his 'bonnie leddy'. Robert, coming home to dinner, sees his violin burning in the fire.

> All its strings were shrivelled up save one, which burst as he gazed. And beside, stern as a Druidess, sat his grandmother in her chair, feeding her eyes with grim satisfaction on the detestable sacrifice.

To appreciate the emotion of this incident we must have seen Robert, as MacDonald has made us see him, making the 'bonny leddy', which had been his father's (whence Mrs. Falconer's fear of its influence), the voice of his soul, a veritable David's harp for godly utterance. He goes to his bedroom presently, after seeing his music-room, the old factory shed, demolished, and cuts loose his favourite kite, his 'dragon', which floats out of his window secured to the bed-rail:

> Whether it was from the stinging thought that the true skysoarer, the violin, having been devoured by the jaws of the firedevil, there was no longer any significance in the outward and visible sign of the dragon, or from a dim feeling that the time of kites was gone by and manhood on the threshold, I cannot tell; but he drew his knife from his pocket, and with one down-stroke cut the string in

twain. Away went the dragon, free like a prodigal, to his ruin. And with the dragon, afar into the past, flew the childhood of Robert Falconer. He made one remorseful dart after the string as it swept out of the skylight, but it was gone beyond remeid. And never more, save in twilight dreams, did he lay hold on his childhood again.

This is true tragedy, for Robert's fiddle had voiced no sin in his hands, and his grandmother was a great-hearted woman and never, for all her austerity, loses our affection. It is her intense desire to save the son from the dangers that had overcome the father that makes her imperil his soul by submitting it to a test which all her moral discipline would never have enabled it to survive, but for that deep and emotional yearning after God which she so misunderstood and distrusted.

§ 4.

Second among the novels I incline to place *Sir Gibbie*. It is not as a whole the equal of *Robert Falconer*. The tendency to melodrama, which extends in the latter book only to the excessive 'make up' of some of the minor characters, notably the more cultured ones, the 'villain', Lord Rothie, and the weak 'heroine', Mysie, here affects the plot. In *Robert Falconer* the improbable discovery of his father does not really affect the fabric of the book. In *Sir Gibbie* the 'missing heir' motive which strains our credulity is the very warp of its material, and the mental and physical accomplishments of *Sir Gibbie,* the dumb, starved uneducated waif, are almost beyond nature.

Yet it is the character of Sir Gibbie, a beautiful and by no means ineffectual angel, that gives the book its great charm, though the idyllic chapters of life on the mountain farm furnish a worthy background. Here too we first meet Donal Grant, the shepherd poet, into whose mouth MacDonald puts some of his best dialect verses, and from no book can more sentences be quoted expressive of his sane and lofty philosophy of life. Sir Gibbie is akin to that great type, Ivan the Fool, the divinely inspired simpleton, who takes Christ's teaching literally and applies it in the workaday world, of which Dostoieffski's *The Idiot* is the most famous example in modern literature. Robert Falconer had something of this quality, but Sir Gibbie, who is of intent made an altogether abnormal person, has far more. Indeed his guardian, the Reverend Mr. Sclater, a good man within limits, has to remove the Bible from his parlour lest his ward be moved to further breaches of the *convenances.*

There is no need to discuss the other novels in detail. Some, *David Elginbrod* for example, and *Alec Forbes,* are little behind the first two. Generally it may be said of Mac Donald as of Scott, that he writes better of Scotland than of England, and that the higher ranks of the gentry appear to less advantage than the peasantry; not because they are intended to have less moral excellence, but because they lack the ruggedness and directness wherein lies the strength of Mac-Donald's portraiture. Similarly his men are better than his women. With children of either sex he is at home, and his old women and sterner peasant types are admirable, but the mature maidens of his stories are a thought too near to 'bread and butter misses' for his sturdy, downright young Scotsmen.

One point in which Sir Gibbie has the advantage over *Robert Falconer* is in the superiority of Ginny over Mysie or Miss St. John. But Ginny is still little more than a child when the book ends, and even she hardly holds her own beside Gibbie and Donal. *Alec Forbes* boasts quite a charming little heroine, but she like Ginny is still in her

teens when we leave her. *David Elginbrod,*
the book by which MacDonald first made his
name, has too much of Bulwer's spurious ro-
manticism, the current influence of the
period in this direction being strengthened
in MacDonald's case by that of his German
master in romantic mysticism, Novalis. The
women here suffer from a double portion of
the defects of the whole book. The first few
chapters, where the scene is laid in the High-
land country-side and in which alone David
appears in the flesh, are by far the best in
the book, and the discerning critic might
have foretold wherein MacDonald's strength
and weakness were to lie.

§ 5.

MacDonald's claims to consideration as a
novelist are great, and it is hence perhaps
that his widest fame must be looked for ; but
he achieved even greater success in another
field. As a teller of fairy stories of two
distinct, though related, kinds he is peerless.
I remember as a boy reading *The Princess
and the Goblins,* and its sequel *The Princess
and Curdie,* and being enthralled by them.
They excited wonder at the events and
admiration for the personages. They are in

fact stories with original and novel plots
(though that is of less importance in a
fairy story than in any other) and characters ; and MacDonald, with his imagination
for ever inspired by the beauty of nature,
imparts loveliness as well to the outward
show as to the inward meaning. Twenty
years later I reread these stories, expecting,
as has, alas, so often happened in like cases,
to be disillusioned. But no, I was as much
charmed as ever. I can only repeat, for to
dissect a fairy story is as unworthy a task
as to explain a jest, that, except by Hans
Andersen, MacDonald is unrivalled as a
modern maker of fairy tales.

The moral beauty of these stories, of which
the child of course is not consciously aware,
lies principally in this—that MacDonald
never lets his allegory obtrude (as Kings-
ley's I fear does in *The Water Babies)* and
that he is content to let us forget it
occasionally to moralize only such parts as
he safely may and to leave the delightful
tale to run its own course. He makes use of
the river ; he does not dig a canal.

At the Back of the North Wind, a tale with
a less romantic setting, lacks this supreme
virtue—it is not a yarn, and appeals to me

least of all the better known fairy tales. The
shorter tales, *The Light Princess* and its
fellows, have all the beautiful imaginative-
ness of *Curdie;* all display MacDonald's
talent for combining mythmaking with pure
story telling, if indeed the story element be
not the prime element in all good myth.

But the greatest of MacDonald's writings
are in that other mode of fairy tale represented by his first and his last prose
books, *Phantastes* (1858) and *Lilith* (1895).
Here the mystic that he always was is in full
control of his invention. Through all his
novels runs this sense of natural things as
symbols of things spiritual—witness the
passage quoted above of the dragon-kite,
emblem of Robert Falconer's passing youth.
He many times asserted the inadequacy of
the material to express the spiritual. Of
Robert Falconer he wrote :

> He saw that any true revelation must come out
> of the unknown in God through the unknown in
> man . . . that only as life grows and unfolds can
> the ever-lagging intellect gain glimpses of partial
> outlines fading away into the infinite—that indeed
> only in material things and the laws belonging to
> them, are outlines possible—even then, only on the
> pictures of them which the mind that analyses them
> makes for itself, not in the things themselves.

In one of his critical essays, he wrote, 'All
that moves in the mind is symbolized in
Nature'; and 'The imagination of man has
the divine function of putting thought into
form'. It 'turns inside out'; and the end of
imagination is 'harmony'. Thus neither simple observation and description of nature, nor
yet reverie—vague and formless dreaming,
—satisfies him. By the exercise of imagination man must reconstruct the world as
God's mind projected it—there lies true
beauty. Also man's physical powers must
serve his imagination, and, working on the
material actually at hand, try to bring the
world up to the ideal.

In all his novels he has this object before
him, to paint the world as it is, but also to
show how much of its spirit is really the spirit
of Christ. In his fairy tales of the first class
he deals still with characters of which even
the supernatural ones are highly anthropo-
morphic, and in any case as real to children
as any other persons in fiction. In the tales
of the second class he gives his imagination
freer play. He is not speaking in allegory so
much as creating or revealing a new world
in which the spiritual is more directly and
clearly bodied forth. 'The imagination of

man has the divine function of putting thought into form '. Which is more, be it noted, than expounding the thought that underlies a sensibly perceived form. He draws a distinction too between *embodying* ideas and merely clothing them in words, which is what Shelley, in his view, too often does.

Phantastes is far the earlier and the better known book. Anodos, the hero, finds his way into Fairy-land, a country which indeed is always with us, concealed as it were in the interstices of this waking world. He takes part in the continual warfare between the spirits of good and evil ; but MacDonald's tales are never oppressively allegorical ; he is rather a maker of myths, fashioning beautiful shapes and living characters, which we feel to be symbols but never *mere* symbols. The tale is always capable of object-ive interest for a child.

Lilith, forty years later, shows even greater skill in this respect. Though the spiritual import is even deeper and more beautiful, it has yet more charm as a story of human adventure in Fairy-land. In the earlier book there is discernible a trace of the artificial, sentimental German romance of Novalis. In

Lilith the poet's imagination creates a new world, clear yet shadowed, filled with strange beasts, a magic, romantic country, yet seeming to show us the reality that lies at the back of our normal world. The wonderful beast Lena and the charming Little Ones are in the most literal sense creations, seemingly natural, yet not with the nature of our waking world. The descriptions of the sleeping of the dead with their first forebears, Adam and Lilith, might have been given visible expression by the imagination of William Blake.

MacDonald is a remarkable blend (much more remarkable from its rarity than such a blend need or should be) of the accurate observer and the visionary. He has painted pictures, faithful in the letter and in the spirit, of Scots peasant life. He has painted other pictures that embody his own spiritual vision. But he never loses sight of the actual in depicting the ideal, nor of the ideal in depicting the actual. There are angels in his kailyards, to those who have the vision to see them. There are human passions in the heart of his mythical creatures. He is a true opener of doors in the wall that divides the material from the spiritual realm. Anodos

and Diamond can find their way into Fairy-
land. So can ministers of grace come from the
spirit world and inform the lives of Sir
Gibbie, of Robert Falconer, of David Elginbrod.

§ 6.

As a poet even more than as a prose romancer, MacDonald's fame falls short of his de-
serts. He had vision, he had interpretive
powers. He chiefly lacks that easy command
of rhythm and harmonious numbers which if
it is the least is at least one of the necessary
attributes of a poet, without which the most
gifted seer cannot make his message ring
home to the hearts of his hearers. There are
lines in MacDonald's verse which have a
most graceful and engaging melody—some
of his songs sing themselves in the true
lyric fashion, witness the well-known

> Alas, how easily things go wrong,
> A sigh too much and a kiss too long;
> And there follows a mist and a weeping rain,
> And life is never the same again.

in *Phantastes,* or

> Love me, beloved, for one must lie
> Motionless, lifeless, beneath the sky;
> The stiff pale lips return no kiss
> To the lips that never brought love amiss;

17

And the dark brown earth be heaped above
The head that lay on the bosom of love.
(Within and Without, Part IV.)

MacDonald's ear was often caught by
beautiful cadences, but it was too little critical and would accept too much that fell too
far short of his own best music. Often, too,
he seems not to have realized that the
rhythm with which a phrase associated itself
in his own ear might not inevitably suggest
itself to another's. He was, one would suppose, a facile writer and, intent on saying his
say, not disposed to any meticulous study of
the technique of his own verse, a weakness
pardonable in a poet who is lyrical always,
who 'pipes but as the linnets do', but serious
in an intellectual who is bent on giving
poetic form to much that does not sing its
own tune but calls for the application of a
deliberate, artistic method.

It is unfortunate too for his fame in the
eyes of the present generation that in his
long poems, as to some extent in his novels,
MacDonald allowed himself to be influenced
by the prevailing fashion of his youth, the
fashion of the 'spasmodics', from which not
even Tennyson or the Brownings kept themselves free. This sort of poetry involved the

use of a rather sentimental and often morbid story, in which the almost inevitable flatness of certain mechanically necessary parts is relieved (or, alas, emphasized) by a use of emotional language that too often rings false—exclamations, sobs, laboured heightenings of style, pathetic fallacies and all the tricks, justified only by a success which leaves the critic breathless, of the poetic trade.

The play *Within and Without,* MacDonald's first poetic fruit, is in parts moving, proceeding from and inspiring genuine emotion. The blank verse is full of colour and variety, but the piece is not designed for the stage and lacks the continuity and single largeness of tragedy, so that it strikes the reader today as prolix, garrulous, and too facile in its handling of passion.

A Hidden Life, which followed, tells us much that is interesting and true concerning the growth of the poetic faculty, but the story is morbid and the manner febrile. Yet it is a better poem than Buchanan's *Idylls* to which (as well as in a less degree to Tennyson's) it bears a likeness.

The Disciple inaugurates a more pronouncedly religious vein in MacDonald's poetry,

17*

and no poet since the 17th century has written on these themes with more passionate sincerity or more adequate mastery of language. Particularly beautiful are some of his sonnets, of which, beginning with those inserted in *Within and Without,* he wrote a large number, striking at times a truly Miltonic chord. In his form MacDonald is deliberately original, employing the Italian scheme of rhyme, but using as a rule two septets instead of an octave and sestet, thus,

THE CHRYSALIS.

Methought I floated sightless, nor did know
That I had ears until I heard the cry
As of a mighty man in agony;
"How long, Lord, shall I lie thus foul and slow?
The arrows of thy lightning through me go,
And sting and torture me—yet here I lie
A shapeless mass that scarce can mould a sigh!"
The darkness thinned; I saw a thing below
Like sheeted corpse, a knot at head and feet.
Slow clomb the sun the mountains of the dead,
And looked upon the world: the silence broke!
A blinding struggle! then the thunderous beat
Of great exulting pinions stroke on stroke!
And from that world a mighty angel fled.

This is not a faultless sonnet. The frequent exclamation marks suggest a jerkiness alien to the true sonnet manner, and 'a blinding struggle' is not a happy phrase. But there is vision, and a volume of sound, and that indefinable quality which stirs emotion.

§ 7.

In everything George MacDonald wrote
and in every faot recorded of his life the
same qualities are manifest, the spiritual
fervour and the intellectual sincerity of the
man. It is in relation to these qualities that
all the characters of his fiction are portray-
ed. Their success or failure in life is measur-
ed by their keeping or losing their hold on
these essentials, and the art of the writer
lies in making his readers accept always his
standard, in compelling their sympathies to
run with his, not with the world's.

To MacDonald, as to his Master, charity is
the greatest of the virtues, and charity is
love and personal service : not love without service nor yet, I think, service without
love ; not the mere giving of alms or a
placid indulgence in platitudes. Every-
where he demands the warmth of the heart
rather than the brilliance of the intellect. He
is for ever denouncing the oratorical fire-
works of the pulpit. It is impossible to read
his reproof of ' the pyrotechnist of human
logic' without remembering the complaints of
his Arundel congregation, who would doubtless have welcomed this very thing, concerning his own doctrinal shortcomings. *Sir*

Gibbie and *Robert Falconer* abound in varia-
tions on this theme, no less than his poetry
which, after all, does but chrystalize the
philosophical teaching of his prose.

As with religious so with mundane knowledge, he mistrusts whatever comes not
from the man himself. Books are an instrument of culture, not a source of opinions. His
ideal scholar is he who, like the hero of
A Hidden Life, uses his book-learning to
deepen and enrich his practical life, who,

Too wise to fancy that a gulf gaped wide
Betwixt the labouring hand and thinking brain,

stayed a farmer all his days and sought only
to be a better farmer and a better man.

It is this passionate devotion to the good
that springs out of a man's own blood that
makes MacDonald, though himself an exile
from his native land, a zealot for the homely
Scots speech, and heats his wrath against
those who from an affectation of gentility
employ in their own homes the tongue of the
Southerner.

If love has the first place in MacDonald's
ethical system, the other two of the trio of
Christian cardinal virtues are not ignored.
Faith and Hope proceed the one from the
other. He who has faith in God cannot lack

hope, and MacDonald has no doubt of the
ultimate triumph of God :

And should the twilight darken into night
And sorrow grow to anguish, be thou strong;
Thou art in God, and nothing can go wrong
Which a fresh life-pulse cannot set aright.
And do not fear to hope. Can poet's brain
More than the Father's heart rich good invent?

(Within and Without, Part IV.)

Work on, one day, beyond all thoughts of praise,
A sunny joy will crown thee with its rays;
Nor other than thy joy thy recompense.

(Within and Without, Part V.)

THE END.